Joseph Ames

An Index to Dibdin's Edition of the Typographical Antiquities

Joseph Ames

An Index to Dibdin's Edition of the Typographical Antiquities

ISBN/EAN: 9783337250966

Printed in Europe, USA, Canada, Australia, Japan

Cover: Foto ©Thomas Meinert / pixelio.de

More available books at **www.hansebooks.com**

INDEX TO
TYPOGRAPHICAL ANTIQUITIES.

An Index to Dibdin's Edition of the Typographical Antiquities first compiled by Joseph Ames, with some references to the intermediate edition by William Herbert.

Printed from a copy in the Library of Sion College.

LONDON:

PRINTED FOR THE BIBLIOGRAPHICAL SOCIETY,

BY BLADES, EAST & BLADES.

—

DECEMBER, 1899.

PREFACE.

This Index to Dibdin's Edition of the *Typographical Antiquities, or the History of Printing in England, Scotland and Ireland,* originally compiled by Joseph Ames, is not a new work, but a reprint of one which exists, so far as is known, only in a single copy, that belonging to the library of Sion College, as to the provenance of which no information can be obtained. The Index has been reprinted at the suggestion of Mr. Gordon Duff, not because it is a good Index, but because the technical defects, which probably account for its never having been put into circulation, are not sufficiently serious to prevent its being a useful makeshift, the publication of which is quite worth the few pounds it has cost to print. Attempts were made to improve it here and there as it passed through the press, but it was found so difficult to alter in one place without altering in another, that it was ultimately decided to let it go forth in its original form.

It has only to be added that the references to Herbert's Edition are distinguished by being enclosed in round brackets.

ALFRED W. POLLARD.

November, 1899.

INDEX TO TYPOGRAPHICAL ANTIQUITIES.

Alexis' Secrets. John Kingston.
1558. 4to. IV. 468n.
1548. 4to. IV. 477n.
n.d. 4to. IV. 484n.
Alexis' Secrets. Hy. Sutton. 1559.
4to. IV. 487.
Alexis' Secrets. Rowld. Hall. 1562-3.
4to. IV. 417.
Alexis' Secrets. John Wight.
1566. 4to. IV. 371.
1578. 4to. IV. 372.
1580. 4to. IV. 373.
n.d. IV. 378.
Allde, Edward. (ii. 1238.)
Allde, John. IV. 571. (ii. 889.)
Almanack. Michl. Lobley. 1545.
fol. III. 539.
Almanack. Hy. Sutton. 1559. 8vo.
IV. 486.
Almanack, Novum. Regd. Wolfe.
1556. 8vo. IV. 24.
Almanack, pleasaunt, for thre yeres.
Thos. Marshe. 1560. 4to. IV.
498.
Almanack, Securis'. 1566. IV.
507.
Almonestry ; place where Caxton
printed. I. xcix. cii.
Alphabetum Lat. Ling. T. Berthelet.
1543. 4to. III. 318.
Ambrose, St., his devout Prayer. John
Cawood. 1555. 8vo. IV. 394n.
Ames, his preface. I. 2.*
Ames, Memoirs of. I. 23* to 51.*
Ames, Criticism on his Typographi-
cal Antiquities. I. 15.* 37.*
Ames, Prospectus of his Work. I. 34.*
Ames, Epistle thereupon. I. 35.*
Ames, his Catalogue of English
Heads. I. 47.* 48.*
Anatomiæ Compend. Delineatio.
Nichs. Hyll. 1552. fol. IV. 233.

Anatomie of a Hand. Wm. Folling-
ham. 1544. 12mo. IV. 38.
Andreæ, Anton. Questiones. John
Lettou. 1480. fol. II. 2.
Andrewe, Laurence. III. 262.
(i. 412.)
Ane Admonition, &c. John Day.
1571. 8vo. IV. 123.
Ane Detection, &c., of Marie Queene
of Scottes. John Day. n.d. 8vo.
IV. 163.
Annibal and Scipio. T. Berthelet.
1544. 4to. III. 324-334.
Annus Quadragesimus. Rt. Redman.
1544. fol. III. 229.
Answer of the Prince of Orange.
John Jugge. 1577. 8vo. IV.
267.
Answer of the Basile Preachers. John
Day. 1549. 8vo. IV. 56.
Answer to the Poysoned Boke. Wm.
Rastell. 1534. 8vo. III. 380.
Answer to a letter. T. Godfray. n.d.
8vo. III. 70.
Answer to Poltrot's Examination.
Rowld. Hall. 1563. 8vo. IV.
419.
Anthony, St., Life of. J. Notary.
[1520.] 4to. II. 584.
Antichrist. Christr. Truthall. 1556.
16mo. III. 60.
Antidotharius, The. Rt. Wyer. n.d.
12mo. III. 187.
Antidotes, holsome. H. Powell.
1548. 8vo. IV. 310.
Antiprognostication. Hy. Sutton.
1561. 8vo. IV. 488.
Antiprognosticon. Hy. Sutton.
1560. 8vo. IV. 488.
Antipus and Antigraphe, a Com-
parison between. John Day. n.d.
4to. IV. 175.

Articles, &c. John Cawood. n.d.
8vo. IV. 404.
Articles. Rd. Grafton.
1548. 4to. III. 458.
1553. 4to. III. 479.
Articles of Christian Faith. Rd.
Jugge. 1548. 8vo. IV. 243.
Articles of Christian Faythe. G.
Lynne. 1548. 8vo. IV. 316.
Articles of Visitation, 1st Eliz. Rd.
Jugge. 1559. 4to. IV. 248.
Articles by Bps. and Archbps. Rd.
Jugge. 1571. 4to. IV. 257.
Articles held at Westminster. Rd.
Jugge. 1575. 4to. IV. 260.
Articles of Kings Counsel. T.
Berthelet.
1533. 8vo. III. 280.
1536. 4to. III. 295.
Articles of our Faith. Rd. Pynson.
n.d. 4to. II. 569.
Articles relating to the Diocese of
Norwich. Regd. Wolfe. 1567.
4to. IV. 31.
Articles relating to the Diocese of
Canterbury. Regd. Wolfe. 1569.
4to. IV. 32.
Articles to be enquired into, &c. John
Kingston. n.d. 4to. IV. 484n.
Articles twelve, Declaration of. G.
Lynne. 1548. IV. 315n.
Articuli, &c. Hy. Smith. 1545.
8vo. IV. 228.
Articuli, &c. Regd. Wolfe. 1550–
1551. IV. 13–19.
1563. 8vo. IV. 27.
Articuli ad Narrat. Nov. T. Berthelet.
1530. 12mo. III. 276n.
Articuli ad Narrationes. Rd. Pynson.
1525. 16mo. II. 512.
Articuli ad Narrat. Novas. Rt. Redman. 1525. 18mo. III. 218.

Articuli inter Archiep. et Epis. John
Day. 1571. 4to. IV. 121.
Arturii Reg. Brit. Assertio. Regd.
Wolfe. 1544. 4to. IV. 8.
Ascensius's Declensions. W. de
Worde. 4to. II. 203.
Ascham's Affairs of Germany. John
Day. 1570. 4to. IV. 118.
Ascham's Schoolmaster. John Day.
1570. 4to. IV. 117.
1570. 4to. IV. 120.
Ascham's Toxophilus. Thos. Marshe.
1571. 4to. IV. 315n.
Ascham's Treatise of Astronomie.
Wm. Powell.
1550. 8vo. IV. 284.
1552. 16mo. IV. 284.
1558. 8vo. IV. 286.
Ashby (Rev. George). I. 64.* xvij.
Askam's Herbal. Wm. Powell. 1550.
8vo. IV. 284.
Askell, Leonard. III. 587 (i. 593).
Aspley. (iii. 1384.)
Assault of the Sacrament. Rt. Caley.
1554. 4to. IV. 459.
Assembly of Fouls. W. de Worde.
1530. fol. II. 278.
Assertio Arturii Reg. J. Herforde.
1544. 4to. III. 555.
Assertion and Defence of Sacrament. J. Herforde. 1546. 8vo.
III. 558.
Assyse of Bread and Ale. Rt. Wyer.
n.d. III. 187.
Astle, Mr. Thomas. I. 66.*
Astley. (iii. 1381.)
Astronomy, Dyfference of. Rt. Wyer.
n.d. 12mo. III. 200.
Astronomy, Boke of. Rt. Wyer. n.d.
12mo. III. 200.
Atkyns, Richard, his work upon
Printing. I. lxxiv. xcvi.

Ballard (Henry). (ii. 1292.) (iii. 1292.)

Bamford, Henry. (ii. 1138.)

Ban Wedy., &c. Rt. Crowley. 1550. 4to. IV. 332.

Bancroft's Translation. John Day. 1548. 8vo. IV. 51.

Banishment of Cupid. Thos. Marshe. 1587. 8vo. IV. 534n.

Banister's Chirurgery. Thos. Marshe. 1575. 8vo. IV. 521.

Bankes, Richard. III. 251. (i. 405.)

Banket of Sapience. T. Berthelet. 1542. 12mo. III. 316. 1545. 8vo. III. 330.

Banket of Sapience. John Day. 1557. 8vo. IV. 67.

Baptisme, Institucion of. Ay. Scoloker. n.d. 16mo. IV. 307.

Barbara, St., Life of. J. Notary. [1518] 4to. II. 584.

Barclay, Alex., Eclogues of. Rd. Pynson. n.d. 4to. II. 557.

Barclay's Egloges. H. Powell. n.d. 4to. IV. 311.

Barclay's Egloges. J. Herforde. n.d. 4to. III. 560.

Barclay's Fifth Eclogue. W. de Worde. n.d. 4to. 387.

Barker, Christopher. (ii. 1075.)

Barker, Robert. (ii. 1090.)

Barley, William. (ii. 1277.)

Barnardine Ochine's Sermons. John Day. n.d. 8vo. IV. 164.

Barnes, Joseph. (iii. 1398.)

Barnes or Bernes, Juliana, Book of Hawking, etc. W. de Worde. 1496. fol. II. 55.

Barnes, Rt., Protestation of. Eliz. Redman. 1540. 8vo. III. 248.

Barnes's Supplication. H. Singleton. n.d. 8vo. IV. 296.

Baro De Fide. Rd. Day. 1580. 8vo. IV. 180.

Bartholomæus de Proprietatibus Rerum, Caxton's edition of. I. xc.

Bartholomæus de Proprietatibus Rerum. W. de Worde. n.d. II. 310.

Bartholomæus de Proprietatibus Rerum. T. Berthelet. 1535. fol. III. 291.

Bartholomew's Hospital, Order of. Rd. Grafton. 1552. 16mo. III. 477.

Barthram (Priest), Boke of. Thos. Raynald. 1549. 8vo. III. 569.

Bartlet, or Berthlet, Wm. (ii. 1202.)

Basil, St., his Exhortation. John Cawood. 1557. 8vo. IV. 398n.

Basil, St., Homelye of. John Cawood. 1557. 8vo. IV. 398n.

Basil (S.), the Great, Letter of Nazaanzen. John Day. n.d. 8vo. IV. 173.

Bassus, (certain notes,) &c. John Day. 1560-5. fol. IV. 77.

Batayle between England and Scotland. Rd. Fawkes. n.d. 4to. III. 361.

Batayle of Egyne Courte, &c. John Scot. n.d. 4to. III. 77.

Bateman's Golden Book. Thos. Marshe. 1577. 4to. IV. 524.

Baterie of the Pope's Batereulx. Rt. Crowley. 1550. 8vo. IV. 332.

Batman's Christial Glas. John Day. 1569. 4to. IV. 112.

Battery, strong against the Idolatrous. Hy. Sutton. 8vo. IV. 489.

Baylie, John. (iii. 1385.)

Bayte and Snare of Fortune. John Wayland. n.d. fol. III. 531.

Bible. Wm. Norton. 1575. fol. IV. 552n.

Bible. Tho. Petit. 1551. fol. III. 513.

Bible. Tho. Raynald. 1550. fol. III. 570.

Bible. Edw. Whitchurch. 1540. fol. III. 484.
1550. 4to. III. 495.
1553. fol. III. 498.

Bible. T. Berthelet. 1540. fol. III. 309.

Bible. Wm. Hill. 1549. IV. 322n.

Bible. Jas. Nicholson.
1537. 4to. III. 51.
1537. 4to. III. 52.
n.d. 4to. III. 57.

Bible. Rt. Redman. 1540. fol. III. 233-235.

Bible. John Wight. 1551. fol. IV. 370.

Bibles, ancient, beautiful editions of. I. xvij. xxxix.

Biblia Pauperum. I. vii.

Biblia Sacra. Wm. Norton. 1592-3. fol. IV. 554.

Bibliæ Sacræ. Tom. I. T. Berthelet 1535. 4to. III. 291.

Binge, Isaac. (iii. 1376.)

Birth of Mankind. Thos. Raynald. 1540. 4to. III. 564.
1545. 4to. III. 566.

Birth of Mankind. (Raynald). Rd. Jugge. 1565. 4to. IV. 255.
n.d. 4to. IV. 266.

Bishop, George. (ii. 1146.)

Black Letter, beauty of the foreign books printed in this character. I. cxxv.

Blanchardin and Eglantine, Caxton's edition of. I. 346.

Blasphemies, Five Abominable, H. Powell. 1548. 8vo. IV. 310n.

Blasphemies of the Masse. Wm. Copland. 1548. 12mo. III. 129.

Blazying Starre, &c. John Kingston. 1580. 16mo. IV. 478.

Blount or Blunt, Edward. (iii. 1382.)

Blower, Ralph. (ii. 1305.)

Blondeville's Morall Treatises. Wm. Seres. 1561. 8vo. IV. 204.

Blundeville's Art of Riding. Wm. Seres. n.d. 8vo. IV. 221.

Blundeville's Fower offices of Horsemanship. Wm. Seres. n.d. 4to. IV. 221.

Boccus and Sydracke. T. Godfray. n.d. 4to. III. 65.

Bochas' Fall of Princes. Rd. Pynson. 1494. fol. II. 404.

Bochas, Tragedies of. John Wayland. 1558. fol. III. 530.

Body of Polyce. John Skot. 1521. 4to. III. 74.

Boetius, Caxton's edition of. I. 303.

Boetius, ancient Latin editions of. I. 303.

Boetius, de Consolatione Philosophiæ. John Cawood. 1556. 4to. IV. 397.

Boke made by a Certayn Great Clerke, or New Idoll and Old Deuyll. Rt. Wyer. 1534. 8vo. III. 178.

Boke of Astronomy. n.d. 12mo. III. 200.

Boke of Distyllacyon. Andwe. Laurence. 1527. fol. III. 263.

Boke of Justices of Peace. Rd. Tottel. 1554. 8vo. IV. 426.
1560. 16mo. IV. 432n.
1566. 8vo. IV. 437.
1569. 16mo. IV. 439.

Boke of Knowledge, to live or die. Rt. Wyer. n.d. 12mo. III. 199.

Borde's Introduction to Knowledge. Wm. Copland. n.d. 4to. III. 158.

Botolphi de Boston Indulgentiæ. Rd. Pynson. 1522. II. 500.

Botoner, *alias* William Wyrcestre, some account of. I. 124.

Bouclier, of the Catholike Fayth. Rd. Tottel. n.d. 8vo. IV. 456.

Bourman, Nicholas. III. 588. (i. 594.)

Bourne, Robt. and Porter, John. (ii. 1270.)

Bowen, John, and John Morris. (iii. 1360.)

Bowen, John. (ii. 1304.)

Bowier, Francis. (iii. 1360.)

Boyle, or Boile, Richard. (ii. 1279.)

Bracton de Legibus. Rd. Tottel. 1569. fol. IV. 440.

Bradford on Election, &c. Rowld. Hall. 1562. 16mo. IV. 415.

Bradford's Fruitfull Treatise. H. Singleton. n.d. 16mo. IV. 299.

Bradford's Godly Treatise of Prayer. John Wight. n.d. 8vo. IV. 378n.

Bradford's Sermons. John Wight. 1574. 8vo. IV. 372. 1581. 8vo. IV. 374.

Bradock, Richard. (ii. 1298.)

Braham, Robert, his Critique on Caxton's Troy Book. I. 23.

Brandon, H. et C., Vita et Obitus, &c. Rd. Grafton. 1551. 4to. III. 474.

Breefe Balet, &c. Thos. Powell. n.d. broadside. IV. 545n.

Breviary of Helth. Wm. Midleton. 1547. 4to. III. 551n.

Brevis et perspicua Ratio, &c. Hy. Sutton. 1558. 4to. IV. 485.

Breue Cronycle of the Bishops of Rome. John Day. n.d. 12mo. IV. 171.

Breuiat Chronicle. John Kynge. 1555. 8vo. IV. 337.

Brice's Register of Martyrs. John Kingston. n.d. 8vo. IV. 484n.

Brief and Pleasaunt Treatise. John Kingston. 1581. 16mo. IV. 479.

Brief Collection of Texts of Scripture. G. Lynne. 1549. 8vo. IV. 317.

Brief Declaration of a Victory, &c. John Cawood. n.d. 16mo. IV. 404.

Brief Examination. Rd. Jugge. n.d. 4to. IV. 265.

Brief Exhortation. John Day. n.d. 12mo. IV. 173.

Brief Introductions. John Day. 1558. 12mo. IV. 70.

Brief Request, &c. John Kingston. 1566. 16mo. IV. 473.

Brief Tables. John Wight. 1574. IV. 372n. 1588. 4to. IV. 378.

Brief and Necessary Instruction, &c. John Awdely. 1572. 8vo. IV. 565.

Brief and Playne Declaration. H. Singleton. n.d. 8vo. IV. 299.

Brief and Playne Introduction, &c. Rt. Crowley. 1550. 4to. IV. 332.

Brief and Profitable Treatise. Wm. Seres. 1570. 8vo. IV. 217.

Brief Chronicle. Thos. Marshe. 1561. 8vo. IV. 499. 1564. 8vo. IV. 501.

Brief Exposition upon the Psalm De Profundis. Wm. Norton. n.d. 8vo. IV. 556.

Caius, De Canibus Britannicis. Wm.
Seres. 1570. 8vo. IV. 217.
Caius, Hist. Cant. Acad. John Day.
1574. 4to. IV. 134-5.
Caius, De Pronuntiatione, &c. John
Day. 1574. 4to. IV. 136.
Caius. On the Sweat. Rd. Grafton.
1552. 8vo. III. 476.
Calender of Scripture. Rd. Jugge.
1575. 4to. IV. 259.
Caley, Robert. IV. 457. (ii. 828.)
Calvin against the Anabaptists. John
Day. n.d. 8vo. IV. 166.
Calvin. Of Offences. Wm. Seres.
1567. 8vo. IV. 212.
Calvin. Catechism. Rowld. Hall.
1562. 16mo. IV. 417.
Calvin. Commentaries. John Day.
1570. 4to. IV. 117.
Calvin. Commentaries. John King-
ston. n.d. 8vo. IV. 483.
Calvin. Foure Sermons. John Day.
1574. 8vo. IV. 134.
Calvin. Institutes. Wm. Norton.
1587. 8vo. IV. 553.
Calvin. Profitable Treatise. Rowld.
Hall. [1561.] 16mo. IV. 412.
Calvin. Sermons. John Day.
1561. 8vo. IV. 79.
1569. 8vo. IV. 112.
Calvin. Sermons. Rowld. Hall.
1561. 16mo. IV. 412.
1562. 16mo. IV. 414.
Calvin. Two Sermons. Wm. Seres.
n.d. 4to. IV. 220.
Cambine's Commentaries. Rowld.
Hall. 1562. 4to. IV. 415.
Camelle's Rejoindre. H. Sutton.
n.d. broadside. IV. 489.
Campensis, Johan. on the Psalmes.
T. Gibson. n.d. 8vo. III. 401.

Campion's Challenge. Thos. Marshe.
1581. 4to. IV. 531.
Car, or Carre, Henry. (iii. 1337.)
Cardanus's Comforte. Thos. Marshe.
1576. 4to. IV. 522.
Cardinal Pole's Oration. Owen
Rogers. n.d. 16mo. IV. 547.
Carey's Herball. Anty. Kytson. n.d.
8vo. IV. 542.
Carion's Chronicles. G. Lynne.
1550. 4to. IV. 317.
Carmeleani, Petri, Carmen. Rd.
Pynson. n.d. 4to. II. 548.
Carminum Genera. W. de Worde.
1525. 4to. II. 259.
Carol of Hunting. W. de Worde.
[1521.] 4to. II. 394.
Carpenter or Bollifant, Edmund. (ii.
1215.)
Carr, Roger. IV. 229. (ii. 707.)
Carre, Nicolas. De Scriptoribus
Britannicis paucitate. Thos.
Marshe. 1576. 8vo. IV. 526n.
Carta Feodi. T. Berthelet. 1543.
8vo. III. 320.
Carter, William. (ii. 1204.)
Carteri Annotationes. Thos. Marshe.
1563. 8vo. IV. 501.
Carving, Book of. W. de Worde.
1508. 4to. II. 133.
Case, John. IV. 356. (ii. 771.)
Castalionis Dialogi sacri. Thos.
Marshe. 1573. 8vo. IV. 517.
Castell of Fayth. Rt. Redman.
1534. 12mo. III. 229.
Castell of Helth. Thos. Powell. n.d.
IV. 544.
Castell of Labour. Rd. Pynson. n.d.
4to. II. 557.
Castell of Labour. W. de Worde.
1506. 4to. II. 127.

Caxton. Extracts relating to his burial. I. cx.

Caxton. His character by Lewis. I. cxii.

Caxton. His Devices. I. cxxviii.

Caxton, Lewis's Preface to his Life of. I. lx.

Caxton, Verses in commendation of. I. lx.

Caxton, Testimonies concerning. I. lxiv. lxxi.

Caxton, Remarks upon an expression used in his History of Troy. I. 20.

Caxton. Specimen of his handwriting. I. 84.

Cebes, The Table of. T. Berthelet. n.d. 16mo. III. 354.

Celius Secundus Curio, &c. John Allde. 1596. 8vo. IV. 575.

Censure of Erasmus. Widow of J. Herforde. n.d. 8vo. III. 561.

Certain Bokes of Skelton's. Rd. Lant. n.d. 12mo. III. 581.

Certain Chapters of Proverbs. Thos. Raynald. n.d. 8vo. III. 570n.

Certain Waies of Ordering Souldiours. John Wight. 1588. 4to. IV. 377.

Certaine Select Prayers. John Day. 1574. 8vo. IV. 138.

Certayne Causes, shewing the Decay of England. H. Singleton. n.d. 8vo. IV. 299.

Certayne Psalmes. Widow of J. Herforde. 1550. 8vo. III. 561.

Certein places out of S. Austen. Wm. Hill. 1548. 8vo. IV. 323.

Certeyne Meditations, &c. John Day. 1548. 8vo. IV. 53.

Cessyons of Parlyament. Rt. Wyer. n.d. 12mo. III. 211.

Chaiselat's Booke of Husbandrie. John Kingston. 1580. 4to. IV. 477n.

Chandos, Sir John. I. 230.

Chapel, in a Printer's Office. I. c.

Chard or Charde, Thomas. (ii. 1194.)

Charles the Great, Life of. Caxton's edition. I. 255.

Charlewood, Alice. (ii. 1105.)

Charlewood, John. (ii. 1093.)

Charlton, Richard. IV. 356. (ii. 771.)

Charter of Romney Marsh. Joan. Wolfe. 1579. 8vo. IV. 37.

Charter, the Great. Thos. Petit. 1542. 8vo. III. 510.

Chartier, Alain, his book called "The Curial," Caxton's edition of. I. 333.

Chartuarye, in English. Nichs. Hyll. n.d. 16mo. IV. 234n.

Chastising of God's Children, Caxton's edition of. I. 356.

Chaucer, Canterbury Tales. Caxton's first Edition of. I. 291.

Chaucer, Canterbury Tales. Caxton's second Edition of. I. 295.

Chaucer, Canterbury Tales. Rd. Pynsons'. n.d. fol. II. 521.

Chaucer, Caxton's character of. I. cxvi. 312.

Chaucer, Caxton's Editions of his Minor Poems. I. 306.

Chaucer, his Prayer or Retraction. I. 293, 294.

Chaucer's Woorkes. John Kingston. 1561. fol. IV. 469.

Chaucer, Workes of. Thos. Petit. n.d. fol. III. 514.

Chaucer, Workes of. John Reynes. 1542. fol. III. 269.

B

Christian Friendship. Abm. Veale.
1586. 8vo. IV. 368.
Christian Instruction. Abm. Veale.
1573. 16mo. IV. 361.
Christian Instruction. John Day.
1565. 4to. IV. 102.
Christian Prayers. John Day. 1569.
4to. IV. 109.
Christian Questions and Answers.
Abm. Veale. 1577. 8vo. IV.
364.
Christian State of Matrimony. Abm.
Veale. 1559. IV. 360n.
Christian State of Matrimony. John
Awdely. 1575. IV. 567.
Christianæ Pietatis Pr. Instit. John
Day. 1578. 12mo. IV. 145.
Christiani Hominis Institut. T.
Berthelet. 1544. 4to. III. 322.
Christiani Hominis Institut. Hy.
Pepwell. 1520. 4to. III. 22.
Christina of Pisa, Moral Proverbs of.
Caxton's edit. I. civ. 72, 276.
Christina of Pisa, Some account of.
I. 75.
Chrisostome, Treatise of. John
Cawood. 1554. 16mo. IV. 393.
Christmas Carol. W. de Worde.
1521. 4to. II. 250.
Christmas Carolles. Rd. Kele. n.d.
8vo. IV. 304.
Christmas Banckette. John Mayler.
1543. 8vo. III. 545.
Chronicle, by Harding. Rd. Grafton.
1543. 4to. III. 446.
Chronicle, by Kelton. Rd. Grafton.
1547. 16mo. III. 455.
Chronicle, by Hall. Rd. Grafton.
1548. fol. III. 461.
1550. fol. III. 466.
Chronicle, Little, at the cost of
Pynson. n.d. fol. II. 563.

Chronicle of England. (Wm. Mach-
linia). n.d. fol. II. 12–29.
Chronicle of England. J. Notary.
[1504.] fol. II. 579, &c.
Chronicle of England. Rd. Pynson.
1510. fol. II. 442.
Chronicle of Fabyan. W. Bonham.
1542. fol. III. 584.
Chronicle of Fabyan. John Reynes.
1542. fol. III. 268.
Chronicle of Yeres. Thos. Petit.
1543. 8vo. III. 512.
Chronicle of Yeres. Wm. Copland.
1557. 32mo. III. 143.
Chroniclers, remarks upon the ancient
English. I. xcvii. Suppl.
Chronicles, Epitome of, by Cooper.
T. Berthelet.
1549. 4to. III. 335.
1550. 4to. III. 353.
Chronicles of England. Caxton's
edition of. I. 85.
Chronicles of England. Antwerp
edition of. 1493. fol. I. 91.
Chronicles of England. W. de Worde.
1497. fol. II. 69.
Chronicles of England. Comparison
of Caxton's edition with an old M.S.
I. 93.
Chronicles of England. Metrical
Romance, so called. I. 99.
Chronicles of England, some ac-
count of the ancient editions of.
I. 57*.
Chronicles of all the Kings. W. de
Worde. 1530. 4to. II. 281.
Chrysostome, St., Homilie of. T.
Berthelet. 1544. 8vo. III. 323.
Chrysostome, St., Sermon of. T.
Berthelet. 1542. 8vo. III. 317.
Chrysostome, St., Sermon of. J.
Gowghe. 1542. 8vo. III. 410n.

Commemoration of Bastarde Edm. Bonner. John Allde. IV. 573n.

Commemoration of the Graces, &c., of God. T. Berthelet. 1540. 4to. III. 311.

Commendations of Matrimony. John Rastell. n.d. 4to. III. 105.

Commentarie on St. Peter and Jude. Abm. Veale. 1581. 4to. IV. 366.

Commentary on St. Paul's Ep. Ephes. Rt. Redman. 1540. 8vo. III. 234. n.d. 16mo. 235.

Commission for sending Caxton to settle a Treatise of Commerce. 1. lxxv.

Common Places. Regd. Wolfe. 1563. fol. IV. 28.

Common Places of Scripture. J. Byddel. 1538. 8vo. III. 394.

Common Places of Scripture. Nichs. Hyll. 1553. 8vo. IV. 234n.

Communion, Order of. Rd. Grafton. 1547. 8vo. III. 457.

Comparison of a Virgin and Martyr, by Paynell. T. Berthelet. 1537. 8vo. III. 297.

Compendiosa Anat. Delin. J. Herforde. 1545. fol. III. 556.

Compendiosa totius Anatomie Delineatio. Thos. Geminie. 1559. fol. IV. 537.

Compendious Treatise, &c. Rt. Stoughton. 1551. 8vo. IV. 313.

Compendium Doctrinæ. Stepn. Myerdman. 1551. 8vo. IV. 354.

Compendium of Rational Secretes. John Kingston. 1582. 16mo. IV. 480.

Complaint of a Lover's Life. W. de Worde. n.d. 4to. II. 372.

Complaint of Grace. Rt. Caley. 1556. 8vo. IV. 462n.

Complaint of Peace. J. Byddel. n.d. 16mo. III. 397n.

Complaint of Peace. John Cawood. 1559. 8vo. IV. 399.

Complaint of the Soul. W. de Worde. n.d. 4to. II. 373.

Composition of the Precious Oil, &c. John Allde. 1574. 8vo. IV. 574.

Compost of Ptholomæus, &c. Rt. Wyer. n.d. 12mo. III. 185.

Concordance of the Bible. G. Lynne. 1550. 8vo. IV. 315.

Concordance of the New Testament. T. Gibson. 1535. 8vo. III. 400.

Confessio Amantis, by Gower. (*See* Gower.)

Confession, Maner and Forme of. J. Byddel. n.d. 8vo. III. 397.

Confession of Faythe. Rowld. Hall. 1561. 8vo. IV. 412.

Confession of the Olde Belefe, &c. Christr. Truthall. 1556. 16mo. III. 60.

Confessor, Life of Edward the, supposed edition by Caxton. I. 342.

Confessyon of the Fayth. Rt. Redman. 1536. 8vo. III. 230.

Confutation of a Popishe Libelle. John Kingston. 1571. 4to. IV. 475.

Confutation of Mishapen Aunswerer. John Day. 1548. 8vo. IV. 52.

Confutation of Popish and Antichristian Doctrine. H. Singleton. n.d. 32mo. IV. 300.

Confutation of the Pope's Bull. John Day. 1572. 4to. IV. 125.

Confutation of XIII Articles. John Day. 1548. 8vo. IV. 55.

Craft to live and die well. W. de Worde. 1505. fol. II. 120.

Cranmer (Abp.) Answer to Gardiner. Regd. Wolfe. 1551. fol. IV. 15.

Cranmer. Articles of Visitation. Rd. Grafton. 1549. 4to. III. 467n.

Cranmer. Answer to Gardiner. John Day. 1548. fol. IV. 156.

Cranmer, Catechism. G. Lynne. 1548. IV. 315n.

Cranmer, Catechism. Nichs. Hyll. 1548. 8vo. IV. 231. n.d. 8vo. IV. 234n.

Cranmer, Submissions. John Cawood. 1556. 4to. IV. 397.

Crato, Greek inscription in honour of. I. 49.*

Crede, Exposytion of. Rt. Redman. n.d. 8vo. III. 243.

Crede of the Old Lawe, &c. Rt. Redman. n.d. 12mo. III. 244n.

Crede, the Commune. Rt. Redman. 1533. 12mo. III. 225.

Creed, or Creede, Thomas. (ii. 1279.)

Cronycle, a Short. J. Byddel. 1539. 12mo. III. 395.

Crowley, Robert. IV. 325. (ii. 757.)

Crowley's Epigrams. Rt. Crowley. 1550. IV. 331.

Crowley's Epigrams. John Kynge. 1559. 8vo. IV. 337n.

Crucifixion, curious ancient cut of. I. viii.

Cunningham's Cosmographical Glass. John Day. 1559. fol. IV. 71.

Curial of Alain Chartier. I. 333.

Curtesy, Book of; or, Little John. Caxton's Edition. I. 309.

Cygnea Cantio. Regd. Wolfe. 1545. 4to. IV. 9.

Cyprian, St., Sermon of. T. Berthelet. 1534. 8vo. III. 287. 1539. 8vo. III. 305n.

Cyte of Ladyes, Boke of. Hy. Pepwell. 1521. 4to. III. 24.

Dalderne, or Daldren, John. (iii. 1357).

Dalrymple, Alexander. I. 66.*

Daniel, Exposition of. Thos. Raynald. 1550. 8vo. III. 570.

Daniell, Dreames of. Rt. Wyer. n.d. 12mo. III. 202.

Danter, John. (ii. 1270.)

Dares, character of the historian so-called. I. 9.

Dauis, Mr. Lockyer. I. 62.*

Dauid's Harpe. J. Gowghe. 1543. 8vo. III. 412.

Dauid's Harpe. John Mayler. 1542. 8vo. III. 544.

Dawson, Thomas. (ii. 1115.)

Day, John. IV. 61. (i. 614.)

Day, Richard. IV. 178. (i. 680.)

Daye of Dome. Rt. Wyer. n.d. 16mo. III. 212.

Dayly Exercise and Experience of Deathe. Rt. Redman. n.d. 8vo. III. 242.

Death and Resurrection of Christ. John Day. n.d. 8vo. IV. 166-7.

Death of the Godly. Rd. Jugge. n.d. 8vo. IV. 264.

Deathe's Proclamation. Abm. Veale. n.d. 8vo. IV. 369.

De Authoritate Pastorum. T. Berthelet. n.d. 4to. III. 350.

Debate between the Heralds. Rd. Wyer. 1550. 12mo. IV. 238.

Decade of Voyages. Rd. Jugge. 1576. 8vo. IV. 261.

De Immensa Misericordia. T.
Berthelet.
1533. 8vo. III. 280.
1543. 8vo. III. 321n.
1547. 8vo. III. 331–339n.
Delectable Demandes. John Cawood.
1566. 4to. IV. 401.
De Libertate Christiani. J. Byddel.
n.d. 8vo. III. 399n.
Demands, Joyous. W. de Worde.
1511. 4to. II. 165.
Demaunds, Boke of. Rt. Wyer.
n.d. 12mo. III. 201.
Demonstratiue Oration, &c. H.
Singleton. n.d. 8vo. IV. 296.
De Morbo Gallico. T. Berthelet.
1533. 8vo. III. 279.
De Naturalibus et Mediis. Rd. Har-
rison 1562. 8vo. IV. 560.
Denham, Henry. (ii. 942.)
De Regis Imperio. T. Berthelet.
1547. 8vo. III. 332.
Dering's Sermon. John Day. n.d.
8vo. IV. 172.
Deryng's Lecture. John Awdely.
1574. 8vo. IV. 566.
Description of Britain, Caxton's
edition of. I. 85–100.
Description of Swedland. John
Awdely. 1561. 4to. IV. 563.
Despauterii Nineviti de Accentibus.
W. de Worde. 1525. II. 259.
Desperation of Francis Spira. Wm.
Norton. 1582. 8vo. IV. 552.
Detection of Dice Play. Rd. Tottel.
1552. 8vo. IV. 424n.
Detection of the Devil's Sophistry.
J. Herforde. 1546. 8vo. III. 557.
De Vera Differentia Reg. Pot. et Eccl.
T. Berthelet. 1538. 8vo. III. 302n.
De Vera Obedientia. H. Singleton.
1553. 8vo. IV. 291.

De Vera Obedientia Oratio. T.
Berthelet. 1534. 8vo. III. 290.
         1535. 4to. III. 292.
Devices used by Caxton. I. cxxviii.
Devices Introduced by Foreign Prin-
ters. I. lvii.
Devil's Sophistrie, Detection of. Rt.
Toy. 1546. 8vo. III. 574n.
De Visibili Rom. Anarchia. John
Day. 1573. 4to. IV. 132.
Devonshire and Cornyshe Rebells.
Edw. Whitchurch. 1549. 12mo.
III. 494.
Devotion, Book of. J. Notary.
1502. 18mo. II. 577.
Devout Prayer. Rt. Redman. n.d.
12mo. III. 241.
Devout Psalmes and Collects. Edw.
Whitchurch. 1547. 8vo. III.
490n.
Dewes, Gerrard. (ii. 940.)
Dexter, Robert. (ii. 1267.)
Diacosia Martyrion. Rt. Caley.
1553. 4to. IV. 457.
Dial of Destinie. Thos. Marshe.
1582. 8vo. IV. 582.
Dial of Princes. Thos. Marshe.
1568. fol. IV. 508.
Diall of Princes. Rd. Tottel.
1568. fol. IV. 438.
1582. 4to. IV. 450.
Diall of Princes. John Wayland.
1557. fol. III. 528.
Dialogue, &c. John Allde. n.d.
IV. 578.
Dialogue about Spirit. and Eccl.
Power. T. Berthelet. n.d. 12mo.
III. 345.
Dialogue, &c., between Curate and
Child. John Wayland. 1537. 8vo.
III. 517.

Diversite des Cours. Rd. Pynson.
1525. 16mo. II. 512.
Divers Truths. Thos. Petit. 1547.
8vo. III. 512.
Dives and Pauper. T. Berthelet.
1535. 8vo. III. 294.
Dives et Pauper. Rd. Pynson.
1493. fol. II. 401.
Dives et Pauper. W. de Worde.
1496. fol. II. 67.
Diuine Meditations. Wm. Norton.
1574. 16mo. IV. 552n.
Diuision of the Law, &c. G. Lynne.
1548. 8vo. IV. 315n.
n.d. 8vo. IV. 321.
Diuersite of Courts. Rt. Redman.
1528. 18mo. III. 215.
Diuersite de Courtz. T. Berthelet.
1530. 12mo. III. 276n.
Diuersite de Courtz. Rt. Redman.
1523. 18mo. III. 215.
Doctor and Student. Wm. Middleton.
1543. 8vo. III. 548.
Doctor and Student. Rt. Redman.
1531. 12mo. III. 221.
Doctor and Student. P. Treveris.
1530. 8vo. III. 41.
1531. 8vo. III. 42.
Doctrinal of Health. W. de Worde.
n.d. 4to. II. 327.
Doctrinal of Princes. T. Berthelet.
1534. 8vo. III. 289.
n.d. 8vo. III. 347.
Doctrinal of Sapience. Caxton's
edition of. I. 266.
Doctrinal of Sapience. Ancient
French editions. I. 274.
Doctrine, &c., for any Christian Man.
T. Berthelet.
1543. 4to. III. 321.
1545. 8vo. III. 330.

Doctrine of Princes. Thos. Petit.
n.d. 8vo. III. 515.
Dolorous Lovers. W. de Worde.
1520. 4to. II. 383.
Donatus Devotionis. John Rastell.
n.d. 12mo. III. 109.
Donatus Minor. W. de Worde.
n.d. 4to. II. 306.
Dore of Holy Scripture. J. Gowghe.
1536. 12mo. III. 405.
1540. 8vo. III. 408.
Dorothy, St., Life of. J. Notary.
[date defaced.] 4to. II. 584.
Drant's Two Sermons. John Day.
1570. 8vo. IV. 114.
Drant's Fruitful Sermon. John Day.
1572. 8vo. IV. 125.
Dredge for Defenders, &c. John
Case. n.d. 8vo. IV. 356.
Duresme, Bp., Sermon of. T.
Berthelet. 1539. 8vo. III. 305.
Dyall of dayly Contemplacion. H.
Singleton. 1578. IV. 292.
Dyaloge of Syr T. More, Knt. John
Rastell. 1529. fol. III. 91.
Dyaloge in Englysshe. Rt. Wyer.
n.d. 12mo. III. 191.
Dyalogues between a Doctor and
Studet. Rd. Tottel.
1554. 8vo. IV. 426.
1569. 8vo. IV. 440n.
Dyenge Well, the Way of. T.
Berthelet. 1541. 12mo. III. 315.
Dyer's Novel Cases. Rd. Tottel.
1585. fol. IV. 452.
Dyer's Table of Reports. Rd. Tottel.
1588. 16mo. IV. 453.
Dyetary of Ghostly Helthe. Hy.
Pepwell. 1521. 4to. III. 23.
Dyetary of Health. Rt. Wyer. n.d.
8vo. III. 192.

England, Nicholas. (iii. 1311.)
English and French, Treatise to
learn. W. de Worde. n.d. 4to.
II. 328.
Engraving, Copper plate, account of
the origin of, abroad. I. iv.
Engraving, Copper plate, account of
the origin of, at home. I. xxiv. ·
Engraving, Wooden Block, account
of the origin of. I. iii. iv.
Engraving, Wooden Block. Reasons
of the decay of the art of. I. xxi.
Engraving, Wooden Block. Remarks
on the cross hatchings in. I. cxxii.
iii.
Ensamples of Virtue, &c. John Tys-
dall. 1561. 8vo. IV. 348.
Enterlude of all Maner of Weathers.
Rt. Wyer. n.d. 4to. III. 189.
Enterlude of Youth. Wm. Copland.
n.d. 4to. III. 168.
Enterlude of Youth. John Walley.
n.d. 4to. IV. 274.
Epistles and Gospelles. R. Bankes.
1540. 4to. III. 254.
Epistles and Gospelles. R. Bankes.
n.d. 4to. III. 258.
Epistles of St. John. Jas. Nicholson.
1537. 16mo. III. 52.
Epistle of St. Paul to the Thessalo-
nians. Jas. Nicholson. 1538.
8vo. III. 57.
Epistle of Peter Martir. G. Lynne.
n.d. 4to. IV. 319n.
Epistles, Two. Wm. Riddell. 1553.
16mo. IV. 406.
Epistola Exhortatoria ad Pacem.
Regd. Wolfe. 1548. 4to. IV. 10.
Epitaph of Bp. Bonner. John Allde.
1569. 8vo. IV. 573.
Epitaph of K. Edward. John
Tysdall. n.d. sing. sh. IV. 351n.

Epitaph vpon the Death of Quene
Marie. n.d. sing. sh. III. 583.
Epitaphia et Inscriptiones lugubres.
John Cawood.
1554. 4to. IV. 393n.
1566. 4to. IV. 401.
Epitome of Chronicles. Thos.
Marshe. 1559. 4to. IV. 498.
Epystles and Gospels. Wm. Powell.
n.d. 4to. IV. 288.
Erasmi Opuscula Varia. W. de Worde.
1519. 4to. II. 233, &c.
1525. 12mo.
1535. 12mo.
Erasmi Parabolæ. Wm. Norton.
1587. 8vo. IV. 553.
Erasmus, Censure and Judgment of.
Rt. Stoughton. n.d. IV. 314.
Erasmus, Epistle of. T. Godfray.
1522. 16mo. III. 62.
Erasmus on the Sacrament. Rt.
Wyer. n.d. 12mo. III. 199.
Erasmus, Paraphrase of. Edw. Whit-
church. 1548. fol. III. 491.
1551. fol. III. 497.
Erasmus, St., Life of. J. Notary.
[1520.] 4to. II. 584.
Erasmus, Sermon of the Child Jesus.
Rt. Redman. n.d. 8vo. III.
243n.
Erasmus, Apophthegmes. John
Kingston. 1564. 8vo. IV. 472.
Erasmus, Epistle to Pellicanus. John
Cawood. 1554. 16mo. IV. 393n.
Esop, Fables of. John Walley. n.d.
8vo. IV. 277.
Esope, Fables of. Wm. Middleton.
n.d. 8vo. III. 554.
Esopi Vita, &c. W. de Worde.
1535. II. 294.
Esop's Fables, Caxton's edition of.
I. 208.

Fitzherbert's Grand Abridgement.
W. de Worde. 1516. fol. II. 210.

Flasket, John. (iii. 1378.)

Fletewood's Eleuchus. Rd. Tottel.
1579. 16mo. IV. 448.

Flores Aliquot Sententiarum. R.
Bankes. 1540. 8vo. III. 254.

Flores Aliquot Sententiarum. Wm.
Copland. 1550. 12mo. III. 131.

Flores Aliquot Sententiarum. Rd.
Kele. 1550. IV. 303n.

Flores Aliquot Sententiarum. Wm.
Middleton. 1547. 8vo. III. 550.

Flores Historiarum. Thos. Marshe.
1567. fol. IV. 507.
1570. fol. IV. 512.

Floures for Latine Spekynge. T.
Berthelet. 1533. 8vo. III. 279.
1544. 8vo. III. 326.

Floures of Terence. T. Berthelet.
1538. 12mo. III. 302.

Flower of the Commandments. W.
de Worde. 1509. fol. II. 135.

Flowers for Latin Speaking. Thos.
Marshe. 8vo. IV. 510n.
1581. 8vo. IV. 528.

Follingham or Follington, William.
IV. 38. (i. 613.)

Following of Christ. John Cawood.
1556. 8vo. IV. 398n.

Folowyng of Chryste. Rt. Wyer.
n.d. 12mo. III. 184.

Forest of Historyes. John Day.
1576. 4to IV. 139.

Foreste of Histories. John Kingston.
1571. 4to. IV. 475n.

Fort against the feare of Death, &c.
Thos. Marshe. 1572. 16mo. IV.
517n.

Fortescu, De Polit, Administ. Edw.
Whitchurch. n.d. 16mo. III.
500.

Fortescue's Lawes of England. Rd.
Tottel. 1567. 16mo. IV. 437.

Foundacion of Rhetorike. John
Kingston. 1563. 4to. IV. 472.

Foundement of Contemplacyon. Rt.
Wyer. n.d. 12mo. III. 204.

Fountain or Well of Life. T. Godfray. n.d. 8vo. III. 71.

Four Leaves of True Love. W. de
Worde. n.d. 4to. II. 382.

Four Notable Histories. Thos.
Hacket. 1590. 4to. IV. 587.

Fox's Actes and Monuments, &c.
John Day. 1562. fol. IV. 87.
1570. fol. IV. 115.
1576. fol. IV. 140.
1583. fol. IV. 161.

Fox's Actes and Monuments, &c.
Rd. Day. 1596. fol. IV. 182.

Francis, St., Life of. Rd. Pynson.
n.d. 4to. II. 538.

Fraternitie of Vacabondess. John
Awdely. 1561. 8vo. IV. 564.
n.d. 4to. IV. 569.

French Hood. John Case. 1551.
IV. 356.

French King's Priuie Counsell's Sen-
tence. John Day. 1566. 8vo.
IV. 105.

Friar and Boy. W. de Worde. n.d.
4to. II. 361.

Friendly Farewel. John Day. 1559.
8vo. IV. 75.

Frithe's Boke, Detection of. T. Berthelet. 1554. 4to. III. 341.

Froissard's Chronicles. Wm. Middleton. n.d. fol. III. 552.

Froissart's Chronicles, translated by
Ld. Berners. Rd. Pynson.
1522[1]. fol. II. 506, &c.

Frontinus, Stratagems of. T. Berthelet. 1539. 8vo. III. 305.

c

Germanes against the Council of Paul III. Jas. Nicholson. 1537. 8vo. III. 53.

Ghostly Father confessing his Child. W. de Worde. n.d. 4to. II. 371.

Ghostly Matters, Book of Divers. Caxton's edition. I. 330.

Ghostly Medycynes. Rt. Redman. n.d. 8vo. III. 242.

Gibson, Thomas. III. 400. (i. 490.)

Gibson's Catechism. Wm. Norton. 1579. 8vo. IV. 552n.

Gilbies' Detection of Gardiner. T. Berthelet. 1547. 8vo III. 333.

Gildas, de excid. et conq. Britan. John Day. 1568. 8vo. IV. 109.

Glasse for Gamesters. John Kingston. 1581. 16mo. IV. 480.

Glasse of Truth. T. Berthelet. n.d. 8vo. III. 349.

Goddes and Goddesses. Rt. Redman. 1540. 16mo. III. 235.

Godet, Goodet or Goodhed, Giles. (iii. 1314.)

Godfray, Thomas. III. 62. (i. 319.)

Godfrey of Boulogne. Caxton's edition of. I. 130.

Godlie Exhortation. John Day. 1549. 8vo. IV. 56.

Godliff, or Godlyfe, Francis. (iii. 1325.)

Godly Admonition. Joan. Wolfe. 1580. 4to. IV. 37.

Godly and Comfortable Conferences, &c. John Awdely. 1574. 8vo. IV. 567.

Godly and Fruitful Sermon. Regd. Wolfe. 1553. 8vo. IV. 21.

Godly and holsome Preseruatyue, &c. Rd. Kele. 1551. IV. 303n.

Godly and Lerned Treatise. T. Berthelet. n.d. 16mo. III. 351n.

Godly Confession. John Day. 1550. 4to. IV. 62.

Godly Consolation, Epistle of. Edw. Whitchurch. 1550. 8vo. III. 495.

Godly Instruction. John Day. 1548. 8vo. IV. 52.

Godly Invective. Rd. Grafton. 1547. 8vo. III. 455.

Godly Meditacion. John Day. 1547. 4to. IV. 50.

Godly Meditations. Wm. Seres. 1567. 8vo. IV. 213.

Godly Newe Short Treatise. Rt. Houghton. 1548. 16mo. IV. 312.

Godly Newe Storie. Wm. Hill. 1548. 8vo. IV. 322.

Godly Preservative, &c. Jas. Burrel. 1559. 8vo. IV. 545.

Godly Treatise on Justification. H. Singleton. 1579. 16mo. IV. 293.

Godlye Prayers, &c. John Awdely. 1576. 8vo. IV. 568.

Gods and Goddesses, Names of. W. de Worde. n.d. 4to. IV. 322.

Golden Book of M. Aurelius. Thos. Marshe. 1556–7, 8vo. IV. 497n.

Golden Boke of M. Aurelius. Abm. Veale.
1557. 8vo. IV. 360n.
1571. 4to. IV. 361.

Golden Chaine, &c. John Allde. 1591. 8vo. IV. 576.

Golden Epistle. W. de Worde. 1530. 4to. II. 284.

Golden Fleece, account of the institution of this Order. I. 53, &c.

Golden Legend. Caxton's edition of. I. cvii. 186–195.

Golden Legend. J. Notary. 1503. fol. II. 578.

Great Turkes Courte. Rd. Grafton.
1542. 16mo. III. 445.

Greate Abridgement. Thos. Gaultier.
1551. 8vo. IV. 343.

Gribalde's Epistle. John Kingston.
1582. 8vo. IV. 481.

Griffith, or Greffyn, William. (ii. 922.)

Ground of Artes. Regd. Wolfe.
1558. 8vo. IV. 24.
1561. 8vo. IV. 26.
1573. 8vo. IV. 34.
1561. 8vo. IV. 12.

Gualtherus Alexandreidos. Rd.
Grafton. 1558. 4to. III. 482n.

Gualtier, Thomas. IV. 342. (ii. 765.)

Gubbin, Thomas. (iii. 1353.)

Guenever, the wife of King Arthur.
I. 249-251.

Guiacum, the Wood so-called. T.
Berthelet.
1536. 8vo. III. 296.
1539. 12mo. III. 305n.

Guiccardin, Historie of. Wm. Norton.
1579. fol. IV. 552.

Guilleville, Guillaume de, Author of
the "Pilgrimage of the Soul." I.
158.

Guiscard and Sigismund. W. de
Worde. 1532. 4to. II. 292.

Gunther's Solymarium, Origin of
Godfrey of Boulogne. I. 136.

Gutenberg, some account of his first
Typographical Essays. I. lxxxvii.

Guy, Earl of Warwick. Wm. Copland.
n.d. 4to. III. 167.

Guy de Roye, some account of. I.
273.

Gwynneth's Playne Demonstration,
&c. Thos. Powell. 1557. 4to.
IV. 543.

Hacket, Thomas. IV. 580. (ii. 894.)

Haddon against Orosius. John Day.
1581. 4to. IV. 158.

Haddoni Lucubrationes. Wm. Seres.
1567. 4to. IV. 211.

Haddoni Poemata. Wm. Seres.
1567. 4to. IV. 212.

Hall, Rowland. IV. 410. (ii. 800.)

Handsom Weapon of a Chrysten
Knight. J. Byddel. 1538. 12mo.
iii. 393n.

Harber of Battails, Caxton's supposed
edition of. I. 277.

Harborough of Christianitie. Thos.
Hacket. 1585. 8vo. IV. 585n.

Harchii, Oratio pro reditu Card.
Pole. John Cawood. 1554. IV.
393n.

Hardie, John. (iii. 1376.)

Harding, Dr., Bull granted to. John
Day. n.d. 8vo. IV. 167.

Harmony of Birds. See Armony.

Harpesfeldi Concio. John Cawood.
1553. 16mo. IV. 389.

Harrington, John, Widow of. (iii.
1309.)

Harrison, Richard. IV. 559. (ii.
883.)

Harrison, John. (ii. 1155 and 1158.)

Harrison, Lucas or Luke. (ii. 924.)

Hart's Orthographie. Wm. Seres.
1569. 8vo. IV. 216.

Haruest is at Hande, &c. H. Powell.
1548. 8vo. IV. 310n.

Harvy, or Harvey, Richard. (iii.
1312.)

Hatfield, Arnold. (ii. 1211.)

Haven of Health. Wm. Norton.
1589. 4to. IV. 554.

Hauking, Hunting, and Fysshynge.
Wm. Copland. n.d. 4to. III.
169.

Hildebrande, Life of. W. de Worde.
1533. 4to. II. 292.
Hill of Perfection (Bp. Alcock). W.
de Worde. 1497. 4to. II. 73.
Hill, John. (iii. 1357.)
Hill, William. IV. 322. (ii. 755.)
Hill's Phisiognomie. Wm. Seres.
1571. 8vo. IV. 218.
Hill's Sermon. Wm. Norton. 1593.
8vo. IV. 556n.
Hilton, Walter, Devout Man, &c.
Rd. Pynson. [1506.] 4to. II. 430.
Hilton, Walter, Ladder of Perfection.
W. de Worde. 1494. fol. II. 36.
Hilyas Knight of the Swan. W. de
Worde. 1512. 4to. II. 168.
Hippocratis Aphorismi. Wm. Seres.
1567. 8vo. IV. 212.
Hiræthoc's British Proverbs. Nichs.
Hyll. n.d. 8vo. IV. 235.
Historie of Man, &c. John Day.
1578. fol. IV. 147.
Historie of the Saracens. Abm Veale.
1575. 4to. IV. 363.
History of Graund Amoure, &c. Rd.
Tottel. 1555. 4to. IV. 427.
History of Guy of Warwick. John
Cawood. n.d. 4to. IV. 404n.
History of Lucres of Scene. John
Kynge. 1560. 8vo. IV. 338n.
History of the Jewes. Rd. Jugge.
1561. 8vo. IV. 252.
1567. 8vo. IV. 255.
1575. 8vo. IV. 260.
Historye of Anniball, &c. Thos.
Marshe. 1561. IV. 499.
Holsome and Catholyke Doctrine.
Rt. Caley. 1558. 4to. IV. 463,
464n.
Holy Goost Tre and XII. Frutes.
Robt. Copland. 1533. 4to. III.
119.

Holy Goost, The XII. Fruytes of.
Rt. Copland. 1535. 4to. III. 120.
Holy Ghost, the XII. Fruits of. Wm.
Copland. 1554. 4to. III. 143n.
Homelies. Rd. Grafton.
1547. 4to. III. 456.
1548. 4to. III. 463.
1549. 4to. III. 467n.
1551. 4to. III. 475.
Homelies. Edw. Whitchurch. 1547.
4to. III. 489.
Homilies. John Cawood. 1556.
IV. 398n.
Homily of Marye Magdalene. Regd.
Wolfe. 1565. 12mo. IV. 31.
Honoure, the Palis of. Wm. Cop-
land. 1553. 4to. III. 136.
Hooke, Henry. (iii. 1360.)
Hooper's Apologie; and Expos. of
23rd Psalm. Thos. Hacket. IV.
585n.
Hooper's Apologye. John Tysdall.
1562. 8vo. IV. 349.
Hooper's Sermons. John Day.
1550. 8vo. IV. 62.
Hope of Health. John Kingston.
1564. 8vo. IV. 473.
Hope of the Faithfull. H. Singleton.
1579. 16mo. IV. 293.
Hoper's Funeral Oration. Thos.
Raynald. 1550. 16mo. III. 570n.
Horace's Art of Poetrie. Thos.
Marshe. 1567. 4to. IV. 507.
Horæ. Caxton's edition of. I. 358.
Horæ. Rt. Toy. 1555. 8vo. III.
576.
Horæ. John Wayland. 1558. 16mo.
III. 529.
Horæ, &c. Rt. Wyer. [1535.] 12mo.
III. 176.
Horæ. W. de Worde. 1502. 4to.
II. 107.

Hyve full of Honyc. Thos. Marshe. 1578. 4to and 8vo. **IV.** 525.

Image of both Churches. Rd. Jugge. n.d. 4to. **IV.** 266.

Image of both Pastoures. Wm. Seres. 1550. 8vo. **IV.** 199.

Image of Governance. Wm. Seres. 1565. 8vo. **IV.** 201.

Image of God. John Day. 1580. 8vo. **IV.** 157.

Image of Nature and Grace. John Day. n.d. 8vo. **IV.** 170.

Immortality of the Soule. John Day. 1581. 8vo. **IV.** 159.

Incarnation of Christ. Edw. Whitchurch. 1549. 8vo. **III.** 495.

Incarnation of Christe. Widow of J. Herforde. 1549. 16mo. **III.** 561.

Indagine's Chiromancy. Rd. Jugge. 1558. 8vo. **IV.** 247.

Indentures. W. Faques. 1505-8. single sheets. **III.** 10.

Infancia Salvatoris. W. Caxton. **I.** 301.

Informatio Puerorum. Rd. Pynson. n.d. 4to. **II.** 545.

Information and Petition, &c. Rt. Crowley. n.d. 8vo. **IV.** 334.

Information and Petition, &c. John Day. 1548. 8vo. **IV.** 53.

Initials, Small, earliest known instance of. **I.** xxvii.

Initials, Capital, their origin and progress. **I.** xxvi., &c.

Initials, Capital, those used by Caxton. **I.** cxxiv.

Initials, Capital, account of grotesque ones. **I.** xxvi. xxxii.

Injunctions. Rd. Grafton. 1547. 4to. **III.** 453.

Injunctions. By Bishop of Coventry, &c. T. Berthelet. 1538. 4to. **III.** 304n.

Injunctions by Shaxton, Bishop of Salisbury. J. Byddel. 1538. 4to. **III.** 394.

Injunctions of the Queen's Majesty. John Kingston. 1583. **IV.** 482n.

Inquisition, Practises of the. John Day. 1568. 4to. **IV.** 106.

Inquisition, Discovery of. John Day. 1569. 4to. **IV.** 110.

Institution of a Christian Man. T. Berthelet. 1537. 4to. **III.** 296.

Institution of Baptism. Roger Carr. circ. 1548. **IV.** 229n.

Institution of Christian Religion. Rd. Harrison. 1561 fol. **IV.** 559n.
1562. fol. **IV.** 560.

Institution of Christian Religion. Regd. Wolfe. 1561. fol. **IV.** 26.

Institution of Christian Religion. Joan. Wolfe. 1574. 4to. **IV.** 37.

Institutions of Laws of England. Rt. Toy. 1546. 8vo. **III.** 575n.

Institutions of the Lawes, &c. Thos. Marshe. 1555–6. 8vo. **IV.** 496.

Institutions of the Lawes of England. Wm. Middleton. 1547. 8vo. **III.** 551n.

Institutions, &c., of the Lawes. Wm. Middleton. 1543. 8vo. **III.** 548.

Institutions of the Lawes. Rd. Tottel. 1570. 8vo. **IV.** 440.

Instruccyon of Christen Fayth. H. Singleton. 1550. 8vo. **IV.** 200.
n.d. 8vo. **IV.** 296.

Instruction for Covetous Men. Thos. Raynald. n.d. 12mo. **III.** 571n.

Instruction of a Christian Woman. T. Berthelet. 1540. 4to. 312n.
1541. 4to. **III.** 315.

Jones, Jhones, or Johnes, William, the younger. (iii. 1320.)

Jones, Death of Agnes. Wm. Seres. 1566. 8vo. IV. 211.

Jordans Medytacyons. Rt. Wyer. n.d. 12mo. III. 205.

Joseph of Arimathea. W. de Worde. n.d. 4to. II. 364.

Joy (Geo.). Declaration of Articles. Rt. Toy. 1546. 8vo. III. 574n.

Joye, George. III. 533. (i. 567.)

Joyfull New Tidynges. John Mayler. n.d. 12mo. III. 545.

Joyfull Newes out of Helvetia. John Allde. 1575. 8vo. IV. 576n.

Joyfull Newes out of the Newe found Worlde. Wm. Norton. 1577. 4to. IV. 551.

Jude, Exposition of Epistle of. J. Gowghe. 1538. 8vo. III. 407.

Judgment of all Vrynes. Rt. Wyer. n.d. 12mo. III. 188.

Judicial of Urines. W. de Worde. 1512. fol. II. 171.

Judson, Thomas. (ii. 1297.)

Juelli, Vita et Mors. John Day. 1573. 4to. IV. 132.

Jugge, Joan. IV. 268.

Jugge, John. IV. 267. (ii. 728.)

Jugge, Richard. IV. 241. (ii. 713.)

Junius, F. De Peccato. Rd. Adams. n.d. 8vo. IV. 558.

Justice of Peace. W. de Worde. 1510. 4to. II. 154.
1515. 4to. II. 154.

Justices of Peas. Rt. Redman. 1527. 12mo. III. 219.
n.d. 8vo. III. 238.
n.d. 8vo. III. 238.

Justification by Faith only. Jas. Nicholson. 1536. 16mo. III. 51.

Justin, by Goldinge. Thos. Marshe. 1564. 4to. IV. 502n.
1570. 4to. IV. 514.

Justyce of Peace. Hy. Smyth. 1545. 8vo. IV. 228.

Justyce of Peace. T. Berthelet. n.d. 8vo. III. 290n.
1539. 12mo. III. 305n.

Justyces of Peas. Thos. Petit. 1541. 8vo. III. 509.

Justyces of Peas. John Skot. 1521. 4to. III. 74.

Juvenalis et Persius. Wm. Norton. 1574. 8vo. IV. 552.

Jyl of Brentford's Testament. Wm. Copland. n.d. 4to. III. 156.

Kalendar of New Legend of England. Rd. Pynson. 1516. 4to. II. 464.

Katherine, Life of. W. de Worde. n.d. fol. II. 328.

Katherine of Senis. W. Caxton. I. 317.

Kearney, William. (ii. 1269.)

Kele, Richard. IV. 302. (ii. 746.)

Keltridge's Exposition and Readynges. Abm. Veal. 1578. 4to. IV. 365.

Kent, ancient inhabitants of. I. lxxv.

Kent, ancient dialect of. I. lxxvi.

Keth's Seeing Glasse. H. Singleton. n.d. 32mo. IV. 300.

Kettle's Sermon at Blandford. John Day. 1571. 8vo. IV. 120.

Key of Philosophie. Rd. Day. 1580. 8vo. IV. 181.

King (R.), Dr.; on Dives and Pauper. Rd. Grafton. 1552. 8vo. III. 477n.

Kingston, Felix. (ii. 1292.)

Kingston, John. IV. 465. (ii. 832.)

Kirkham, Henry. (iii. 1321.)

Latimer, Hugonis, Concio. J.
Gowghe. 1537. 8vo. III. 406.
Latimer, Sermon of. T. Berthelet.
1537. 8vo. III. 297.
Latimer, Sermon of. John Day.
  1547. 8vo. IV. 51.
  1548. 8vo. IV. 55.
  1549. 8vo. IV. 57.
  1550. 8vo. IV. 60.
  1562. 4to. IV. 94.
  1571. 4to. IV. 123.
  1578. 4to. IV. 151.
  1584. 4to. IV. 161.
  n.d. 8vo. IV. 174.
Laudatio Pacis. Regd. Wolfe. 1546.
4to. IV. 9.
Laurent De Premier-Faict, short account of. I. 123.
Lawe, Thomas. (ii. 1352.)
Law Tracts. T. Berthelet. 1544.
8vo. III. 327.
Law Tracts. John Rastell. n.d.
16mo. III. 109.
Laws, Customs, &c., of England. R.
Bankes. 1540. 12mo. III. 255.
      1542. 8vo. III. 256.
Lawes and Statutes of Liveries. Rd.
Tottel. 1573. 8vo. IV. 441n.
Lawes, &c., of Geneva. Thos.
Hacket. 1562. IV. 582n.
Lawes of Geneva. Rowld. Hall.
1562. 16mo. IV. 413.
Learnynge, Olde and Newe Companion of. Jas. Nicholson. 1537.
8vo. III. 53.
Leaver's Sermons. John Day. 1550.
8vo. IV. 61.
Leeke, or Leake, William. (iii. 1370.)
Leeu, Gerard, his edition of Caxton's
Chronicles. I. 91.
Leeu, Gerard, his edition of the
Knight Paris. I. 262.

Legate, or Legatt, John. (iii. 1418.)
Legende, Francisci. Hy. Pepwell.
n.d. 8vo. III. 27.
Legibus Angliæ, de. Rd. Tottel.
1583. 8vo. IV. 451.
Lelandi Bononia Gallomastrix. John
Mayler. 1545. 4to. III. 545n.
Lelandi Nœnia. John Mayler. 1544.
4to. III. 545n.
Le Livre de Priers. Thos. Gualtier.
1553. 8vo. IV. 343.
Les Eclaircissements De la Langue Fr.
J. Haukins. 1530. fol. III. 364.
Letany. Thos. Petit. 1546. 8vo.
III. 512.
Letany, Engl. Lat. Rd. Grafton.
1544. 8vo. III. 450.
1545. 4to. III. 450.
Letter, Copie of, from the Council.
John Cawood. 1554. IV. 391.
Letter, Godly, to the fayethfull in
London. H. Singleton. 1554.
8vo. IV. 291.
Letter in vindication of Q. Elizabeth.
Rd. Grafton. 1571. 8vo. III.
482n.
Lettou, John. II. 1. (i. 111.)
Lettou and Machlinia. II. 4. (i. 111.)
Lever's Sermons. John Kingston.
1572. 8vo. IV. 475.
Lewis, John, character of his Life of
Caxton. I. lx., lxxiv.
Lewis, John, account of his publications. I. 30.*
Lewis, John, his correspondence with
Ames. I. 33.*
Lewis, John, his opinion of Bagford.
I. 67.*
Libellus Sophistarum. Rd. Pynson.
1524. 4to. II. 511.
Libellus Sophistarum. W. de Worde.
1510. 4to. II. 152.

Lorde's Supper, Vnderstandinge of the. Wm. Copland. 1548. 8vo. III. 129.

Lorde's Supper, Song of. Wm. Copland. n.d. 4to. III. 151.

Lort, Dr. Michael. I. 64*.

Love, Image of. W. de Worde. 1525. 4to. II. 255.

Lowe Countrey, Things done in the. John Day. n.d. 16mo. IV. 164.

Lownes, Humphrey. (iii. 1367.)

Lownes, Matthew. (iii. 1379.)

Lownes, William. (iii. 1360.)

Lucidary. Wm. Caxton. I. 343.

Lupset, Thomas, Works. T. Berthelet. 1546. 12mo. III. 331.

Lupset, Thomas, Works. John Kynge. 1560. 8vo. IV. 337.

Lust, Thomas. (ii. 1260.)

Lusty Iuventus. Abm. Veale. n.d. 4to. IV. 368.

Luther; Controversial Tracts with Hen. VIII. Rd. Pynson. 1521. 4to. II. 484, &c.

Luther; on the xxiii.rd Psalm. Jas. Nicholson. 1537. 16mo. III. 54.

Luther; Exposition of the 130th Psalm. H. Singleton. 1577. 8vo. IV. 292n.

Luther; Sermon. John Day. 1570. 8vo. IV. 165. 1578. 8vo. IV. 149.

Luther; Sermon, on the Angelles. H. Singleton. n.d. 8vo. IV. 296n.

Lydgate. Wm. Caxton. I. 306.

Lydgate; Testament of. Rd. Pynson. n.d. 4to. II. 545.

Lydgate; Bochas. John Wayland. 1550. fol. III. 520.

Lydgate; Fall of Princes. Rd. Tottel. 1554. fol. IV. 425.

Lydgate; Daunce of Machabree. Rd. Tottel. 1554. fol. IV. 425.

Lyndewode, Const. Provin. Rd. Pynson. n.d. 8vo. II. 539.

Lyndewode, Const. Provin. W. de Worde. 1496. 8vo. II. 52.

Lyndewodi Constitutiones. Thos. Marshe. 1557. 8vo. IV. 497.

Lynge, or Ling, Nicholas. (iii. 1340.)

Lynne, Gualter. IV. 315. (ii. 752.)

Lysons, Messrs. Daniel and Samuel. I. 21.*

Lyttleton's Tenures. Wm. Middleton. 1544-5. 8vo. III. 549.

Lyttleton's Tenures. Thos. Petit. n.d. 8vo. III. 515.

Lyttleton's Tenures. Fr. Rt. Redman. n.d. fol. III. 236.

Lyttleton's Tenures. Eng. Rt. Redman. n.d. 32mo. III. 239.

Lyttleton's Tenures. Hy. Smyth. 1545. 4to. IV. 227.

Lyttleton (*See* Littleton.)

Macer's Herbal. Rt. Wyer. n.d. 12mo. III. 192.

Machlinia, William. II. 8. (i. 112.)

Madeley, Roger. IV. 456. (ii. 827.)

Magliabechi, his early attachment to Literature. I. 74.*

Magna Carta. T. Berthelet. 1531. 8vo. III. 277. 1540. 16mo. III. 309.

Magna Carta. Rt. Redman. 1525. 12mo. III. 215. 1529. 16mo. III. 217. 1534. 8vo. III. 229. 1539. 12mo. III. 232.

Magna Carta. Eliz. Redman. n.d. 8vo. III. 249.

Magna Charta. Thos. Marshe. 1556. 8vo. IV. 496.

Martir, Peter, Commentaries of. John Day. 1564. fol. IV. 100.
1568. fol. IV. 107.
Martyris Loci Comunes. John Kingston. 1576. fol. IV. 476.
Martyr's Godly Prayers. Wm. Seres. 1569. 8vo. IV. 216.
Martyrs; Letters of Holy. John Day. 1564. 4to. IV. 101.
Mass, of the negligences happening therein, and of the remedies. I. 268.
Masse, Interpretacyon, &c, of the. Rt. Wyer. 1533. 8vo. III. 176.
Masse, Treatise against. Thos. Raynald. 1548. 16mo. III. 566.
Mastricht, Report of Assault of. Rd. Adams. 1579. IV. 558.
Mather, John. IV. 562. (ii. 884.)
Mattes, or Matts, Edmund. (iii. 1374.)
Mattes, or Matts, William. (iii. 1375.)
Matthæi Paris, Historia Major. Regd. Wolfe. 1571. fol. IV. 33.
Maundeville, .Travels of. Rd. Pynson. n.d. 4to. II. 568.
Maunsell, Andrew. (ii. 1134.)
Maximilian, Triumphs of the Emperor —a work so-called. I. xxiv.
Mayden's Crosse Rewe. Rt. Wyer. n.d. 4to. III. 208.
Mayden's Dreme. Rt. Wyer. n.d. 4to. III. 208.
Maylard, Leonard. (iii. 1316.)
Mayler, John. III. 541. (i. 570.)
Measures and Weights, &c. Nichs. Hyll. n.d. 8vo. IV. 234n.
Measuring of Lande. Jas. Nicholson. n.d. 16mo. III. 58.
Medicinable Moral. Thos. Marshe. 1566. 4to. IV. 505.

Medicines, approved, &c. Thos. Marshe. 1580. 16mo. IV. 527.
Medicines, Boke of. Wm. Middleton. 1544. 8vo. III. 548.
Medicines, Boke of. Hy. Tab. n.d. 8vo. III. 502.
Medicines, Boke of. King Bocchus. Rt. Redman. n.d. 4to. III. 243.
Meditacion upon the Lord's Praier. John Day. 1551. 12mo. IV. 66.
Meditations, &c. John Allde. n.d. 8vo. IV. 577.
Medius, Morning and Evening Prayer. John Day. 1565. fol. IV. 102.
Medled Lyfe. Rt. Wyer. n.d. 12mo. III. 206.
Melancthon, considering of the Interim. Edw. Whitchurch. 1548. 8vo. III. 492n.
Memento Mori. John Tysdall. n.d. broadside. IV. 351n.
Mercers, some account of the ancient character of. I. lxxviii.
Merchantes, the Booke of. T. Godfray. n.d. 8vo. III. 69.
Merchants, Book of. Rd. Jugge. 1548. 8vo. IV. 243.
Merlin's Prophecy. W. de Worde. 1510. 4to. II. 158.
Merry Jest, &c. John Allde. n.d. 4to. IV. 577.
Merry Prognostication. W. de Worde. n.d. 4to. II. 366.
Message to the People in Devonshire. Rd. Grafton. 1549. 8vo. III. 467n.
Messe, Mother, Indictment against. Wm. Seres. 1548. 8vo. IV. 198.
Method of Wrytyng Histories. Wm. Seres. 1574. 8vo. IV. 219.

D

Modus tenend. Unum. Hund. Rd.
Pynson. n.d. 4to. II. 459.
Modus tenend. Unum. Hund. Rt.
Redman.
1527. 12mo. III. 218n.
n.d. 8vo. III. 239.
Monasteries, account of printing in
them. I. ci.
Monday, Ant; Godly Exercises, &c.
Thos. Hacket. 1586. 8vo. IV.
585n.
Monstrous Broods. I. 139.
Montagu, Earl of Salisbury. I. 230.
Moptid, David. IV. 562. (ii.
884.)
Moral Methode of Ciuile Pollicie.
Thos. Marshe. 1576. 4to. IV.
522.
Moral Play of Every Man. Rd.
Pynson. n.d. 4to. II. 565.
Morall Playe of Euery Man. John
Skot. n.d. 4to. III. 78.
Morbus Gallicus, Cure of. John Day.
1579. 8vo. IV. 155.
More, Apologye of. W. Rastell.
1533. 12mo. III. 377.
More, Bishop of Ely. I. 63.*
More, Dyalogue of. Wm. Rastell.
1531. fol. III. 373.
More, Sir T., Workes of. J. Cawood.
1557. fol. IV. 398n.
More, Sir T., Workes of. Rd. Tottel.
1557. fol. IV. 430.
More, Sir T., Workes of. John
Walley. 1557. fol. IV. 273.
More's, Edward Rowe, cause of his
antipathy to Ames. I. 44.*
More's Utopia. Abm. Veale.
1551. 8vo. IV. 359.
1556. 8vo. IV. 360.
Mori Epistola ad Germanum Brixium.
Rd. Pynson. 1520. 4to. II. 483.

Moriæ Encomium. T. Berthelet.
1549. 4to. III. 335.
Morisin, R. Invective against secret
practices. T. Berthelet. 1539.
12mo. III. 304.
Morisin, R. Exhortation to stir up,&c.
T. Berthelet. 1538. 4to. III. 304n.
Morley, Lord, Declaration of Ps. 94.
T. Berthelet. 1539. 8vo. III. 305n.
Morris, John, and John Bowen. (iii.
1360.)
Morysini Apomaxis. T. Berthelet.
1537. 8vo. III. 298.
Most faithful Sermon. John Day.
1550. 8vo. IV. 160.
Moste Necessary Treatise, &c. John
Tysdall. n.d. 8vo. IV. 352.
Muster of Schismatic Bishops. W.
de Worde. 1534. 8vo. II. 293.
Muster of Schismatike Bishops.
J. Byddel. n.d. 8vo. III. 398.
Mycha, Commentarye upon. John
Day. 1551. 8vo. IV. 66.
Mychell, John. (iii. 1452.)
Myerdman, Stephen. IV. 354. (ii.
770.)
Myroure, or Glasse, &c. Rt.
Crowley. 1551. 8vo. IV. 333.
Myrrour for Magistrates. Thos.
Marshe. 1559. 4to. IV. 497.
1563. 4to. IV. 501.
1571. 4to. IV. 515.
1575. 4to. IV. 520.
1578. 4to. IV. 525.
Myrrour for Sacrament of Baptism.
John Day. n.d. 8vo. IV. 175.
Myrrour of Christes Passion. Rt.
Redman. 1533. fol. III. 225.
Myrrour of Golde. John Skot. 1522.
4to. III. 75.
Myrrour, &c., of Helth, &c. Wm.
Middleton. n.d. 8vo. III. 552n.

Next way to Heaven. W. de Worde. n.d. 4to. II. 332.
Nichodemus's Gospel. J. Notary. [1507.] 4to. II. 581.
Nichodemus's Gospel. W. de Worde. 1509. 4to. II. 144.
Nicholson, James. III. 51. (iii. 1447.)
Nigramansir. W. de Worde. 1504. 4to. II. 119.
Noblenes, Boke of. Rt. Wyer. n.d. 12mo. III. 198.
Nobles, the, or of Nobilitie. Thos. Marshe. 1563. 16mo. IV. 500.
Northumberland, Saying of the Duke of. John Cawood. 1553. 8vo. IV. 389n.
Norton, Thos., his Treatises. John Day. n.d. 8vo. IV. 174.
Norton, Bonham. (ii. 1302.)
Norton, John. (ii. 1296.)
Norton, William. IV. 549. (ii. 877.)
Notable Chapytres. Rt. Wyer. n.d. 12mo. III. 205.
Notable Collection of Scriptural Places. Wm. Seres. n.d. 12mo. IV. 222. 1548. 8vo. IV. 198.
Notable Example of God's Vengeance. John Day. n.d. IV. 162.
Notable Textes of Scripture, &c. Rt. Stoughton. n.d. 16mo. IV. 312.
Notable Treatise on Eating Meats. Rt. Stoughton. n.d. 8vo. IV. 314.
Notary, Julian. II. (i. 475. i. 303.)
Nouae Narrationes. Rt. Redman. n.d. fol. III. 237.
Nouae Narrationes, &c. Rd. Tottel. 1561. 16mo. IV. 432n.

Nova Legenda Anglie. W. de Worde. 1516. fol. II. 209.
Novelle Natura Brevium. Rd. Tottel. 1567. 8vo. IV. 437n.
Nychodemus Gospell. John Skot. 1529. 4to. III. 75. n.d. 4to. III. 77.
Obedience of a Christian Man. Wm. Middleton. n.d. 8vo. III. 553n.
Obedience of a Christian Man. Thos. Raynald. n.d. 8vo. III. 571n.
Obedience of a Christian Man. Wm. Hill. n.d. 4to. IV. 323. n.d. 8vo. IV. 323n.
Obedyence of a Chrysten Man. Wm. Copland. 1561. 8vo. III. 144. n.d. 12mo. III. 146.
Ocham's Dialogue between a Knight and Clerke. T. Berthelet. 1540. 8vo. III. 311.
Ochine's Sermons. Wm. Riddell. n.d. 8vo. IV. 408.
Ockould, or Ockolde, Richard. (iii. 1381.)
Oecolampadius' Sermon. H. Powell. n.d. 8vo. IV. 311.
Oecolampadius' Sermon. H. Singleton. n.d. 8vo. IV. 299.
Office of a Husband. John Cawood. n.d. 16mo. IV. 404.
Office of Sheriffes, &c. John Allde. 1573. 8vo. IV. 574n.
Office of Shiriffes. Thos. Marshe. n.d. 8vo. IV. 534n.
Offices of Sheryffes. Wm. Middleton. 1545. 12mo. III. 549.
Offices of Sheryffes. Rt. Redman. n.d. 8vo. III. 237.
Officials, Collection of. Thos. Raynald. n.d. 8vo. III. 571n.

Offspring of the House of Ottomano.
Thos. Marshe. n.d. 8vo. IV. 534n.
Offyce of Shyryffes. John Kynge.
n.d. 8vo. IV. 340.
Olde and Newe God. J. Byddell.
1534. 8vo. III. 385.
Olde Learnyng and New compared.
Rt. Stoughton. 1548. 8vo. IV.
312.
Oldys, Character of his Life of
Caxton. I. lxxiv.
Oliffe, or Olive, Richard. (iii. 1361.)
Oliver of Castille. (Romance of.)
W. de Worde. 1518. 4to. II.
225.
Olney, Henry. (iii. 1380.)
Omelia Origenis. W. Faques. n.d.
8vo. III. 11.
Onosandro Platonico. Wm. Seres.
1563. 8vo. IV. 209.
On the Supper of the Lord. John
(sic) Turk. n.d. 8vo. IV. 357.
Opus Eximium, &c. T. Berthelet.
1534. 4to. III. 287.
Opusculum De Mort. Resurrect. J.
Herforde. 1545. 4to. III. 556.
Orarium. Rd. Gratton. 1546. 12mo.
III. 452.
Orarium seu Libellus Precationum.
Wm. Seres. 1560. 8vo. IV. 203.
Oratio Jesu Christi. Regd. Wolfe.
1555. 8vo. IV. 22.
Oratio Pia, Religiosa, &c. Wm.
Seres. 1568. 4to. IV. 214.
Oration of Beza. Rd. Jugge. 1561.
8vo. IV. 253.
Orationes Tres. Rt. Caley. n.d.
broadside. IV. 464n.
Orations of Arsanes. John Day.
n.d. 8vo. IV. 162.
Orchard of Sion. W. de Worde.
1519. fol. II. 237.

Ordenarye of Christians. Ay.
Scoloker. n.d. IV. 308.
Ordenarye for Faythful Christians.
Wm. Seres. n.d. 8vo. IV. 225.
Order of Chivalry. Wm. Caxton.
I. 221.
Order of Chivalry. French MSS.
Romance. L. 366.
Order of Common Prayer. Nichs.
Hyll. n.d. 4to. IV. 234n.
Order of Lorde Maior, &c. H.
Singleton. 1586. 8vo. IV. 295.
Order of Matrimony, &c. Ay.
Scoloker. n.d. 16mo. IV. 308.
Orders to be executed in the Cittie
of London. H. Singleton. 4to.
IV. 297.
Ordinance, Copy of the. T. Berthelet.
1544. 8vo. III. 328.
Ordinary for Christians. Thos.
Marshe. 1578. 16mo. IV. 526n.
Ordinary of Christian Men. W. de
Worde. 1502. 4to. II. 101.
Ordynaries. Eliz. Redman. 1541.
8vo. III. 248n.
Ordre of the Almose at Lyons. Edw.
Whitchurch. 1540. 12mo. III.
485n.
Ordre or Trayne of Warre. Rt.
Wyer. n.d. 12mo. III. 207.
Original of Sectes and Orders. J.
Gowghe. 1537. 8vo. III. 407.
Ortus Vocabulorum. W. de Worde.
1500. 4to. II. 88.
Orwin, Joan. (ii. 1249.)
Orwin, Thomas. (ii. 1241.)
Osorius, of Nobilitie. Thos. Marshe.
1576. 4to. IV. 523.
Oswen, John. (iii. 1458 and 1459.)
Otto Brunsfelsius. J. Byddel. 1536.
8vo. III. 393.

Ouersight and Deliberation on Jonas.
John Tysdall. 1550. 8vo. IV.
345.
Ouerthrow of Justification of Works.
John Tysdall. 1561. 8vo. IV.
349.
Ouerthrow of the Gowte. Abm.
Veale. 1557. 8vo. IV. 364n.
Overton, John. (iii. 1456.)
Ovid, Metamorphoses of. Supposed
MS. by Caxton. I. civ. 83.
Oxenbridge, John. (iii. 1368.)
Oxford, book printed at. A.D. 1468.
I. lxxv.
Oxon. Acad. Assert. Antiquitatis.
John Day. 1568. 4to. IV. 109.
1574. 4to. IV. 135.

Pacei Oratio. Rd. Pynson. 1518.
4to. II. 477.
Pageant of Popes. Thos. Marshe.
1574. 4to. IV. 519.
Pain and Sorrow of Evil Marriage.
W. de Worde. n.d. 4to. II. 387.
Painter's Palace of Pleasure. Thos.
Marshe. 1566. 4to. IV. 510n.
1569. 4to. IV. 511.
Palfreyman's Exhortation. Michl.
Lobley. 1560. 8vo. III. 539.
Palfreyman's Paraphrase, &c. Wm.
Norton. n.d. 4to. IV. 556n.
Pallengenii Zodiacus Vitæ. Thos.
Marshe. 1574. 8vo. IV. 517n.
Palmer's History of Printing. I.
lxxiv. 33.*
Palsgrave in Comædiam Acolasti.
T. Berthelet. 1540. 4to. III.
308.
Pandectæ Locorum Communium.
H. Singleton. 1585. fol. IV. 295.
Pandectes of the Ev. Lawe. Nichs.
Hyll. 1553. 8vo. IV. 234n.

Pandectes of the Evangelical Law.
Abm. Veale. 1553. IV. 360n.
Pandects of the Evangelical Law.
Wm. Seres. 1553. 8vo. IV. 200.
Paper, Origin of. I. cxxv.
Paper Mill and Manufactory, first
established in England. I. 56.*
Papists, muttering of, in corners. T.
Berthelet. 1534. 8vo. III. 290.
Parable of the Wycked Mammon.
John Day. 1547. 12mo. IV. 49.
Parabola Alani. W. de. Worde.
1508. 4to. II. 132.
1525. II. 259.
Paradyse of Daynty Devises. Hy.
Disle. 1576. 4to. IV. 187.
1577. 4to. IV. 188.
1578. 4to. IV. 189.
Pardon and Absolution. Rd. Fawkes.
n.d. single sheet. III. 360.
Pardoner and the Frere. Wm. Ras-
tell. 1553. 4to. III. 376.
Paris, The Knight and Fair Vienne.
Wm. Caxton. I. 261.
Paris, The Knight and Fair Vienne.
French editions of. I. 262.
Parker, Abp., Strype's Life of. I. 61.*
Parker, Mr. Henry. I. 62.*
Parker (Bp.), De Antiquitate Brit.
Eccl. John Day. · 1572. fol. IV.
126.
Parkins, Explanatio Capitulorum.
Rt. Redman. 1532. 8vo. III.
223.
Parkins, J. Tractatus. Hy. Smyth.
1545. 8vo. IV. 228.
Parliament, Acts of. J. Notary.
1507. 4to. II. 581.
Parliament of Devils. W. de Worde.
1509. 4to. II. 143.
Parvus Libellus, &c. Rd. Kele.
1546. 8vo. IV. 302.

Parvus Libellus, &c. Rt. Redman.
  1527. 12mo. III. 219.
  1530. 12mo. III. 236.
Pasquil the Playne. T. Berthelet.
  1533. 8vo. III. 283.
  1540. 12mo. III. 307.
Pasquin, Recantation of. John
  Day. 1570. 8vo. IV. 119.
Pasquine in a Traunce. Wm. Seres.
  n.d. 4to. IV. 220.
Passage of Q. Elizabeth to her Coro-
  nation. Rd. Tottel. 1558. 4to.
  IV. 431.
Passage of Q. Elizabeth through
  London. Rd. Grafton. 1558.
  4to. III. 482n.
Passion of our Lord. W. de Worde.
  1521. 4to. II. 246.
Pastime of Pleasure. W. de Worde.
  1517. 4to. II. 211.
Pastyme of People. John Rastell.
  1529. folio. III. 91.
Pater Noster, &c. J. Byddel. 1537.
  8vo. III. 393.
Pater Noster. W. de Worde. n.d.
  4to. II. 323.
Pater Noster of the Sinner. T.
  Godfray. n.d. 8vo. III. 71.
Pater Noster, Paraphrase of. Rt.
  Redman. n.d. 4to. III. 244.
Pater Noster, the Crede, &c. Thos.
  Petit. 1538. 8vo. III. 508.
Pater Noster, Treatise upon. T.
  Berthelet. n.d. 4to. III. 342.
Path of Obedience. John Wayland.
  n.d. 8vo. III. 532.
Pathewaye to a Vertues Lyfe. Nichs.
  Hyll. n.d. 4to. IV. 235.
Pathose, or Passion of the Pope for
  the Losse of his Daughter. John
  Day. n.d. 8vo. IV. 171.

Pathway into the Scripture. T. God-
  fray. n.d. 8vo. III. 71.
Pathway to Knowledge. Rt. Crowley.
  1550. 8vo. IV. 331.
Pathway to Knowledge. Regd. Wolfe.
  1551. 4to. IV. 16.
Pathway to Military Practise. Rt.
  Walley. 1587. 4to. IV. 280.
Pathway (New) unto Prayer. J.
  Gowghe.
  1542. 12mo. III. 410n.
  1543. 8vo. III. 411.
Patricke's Places of Scripture. Wm.
  Norton. 1578. 8vo. IV. 552n.
Patten's Expedition into Scotland.
  Rd. Grafton. 1548. 8vo. III. 458.
Pavier, Thomas. (iii. 1363.)
Paules Accidence. Hy. Pepwell.
  1539. 4to. III. 26.
Paynell; Sayinges of Scripture. Rd.
  Jugge. n.d. IV. 263.
Paynell, Collection of Scripture Say-
  ings. Wm. Copland.
  1560. 12mo. III. 143n.
  n.d. 12mo. III. 145.
Peas, Justice of the. Rt. Copland.
  1515. 4to. III. 113.
Pedegrewe of Popish Heretiques.
  Thos. Marshe. 1566. 4to. IV.
  510n.
Pembroke, Earl of, his Cabinet of
  Coins. I. 47.*
Pendleton's Declaration. Rt. Caley.
  1557. 4to. IV. 463.
Penne, or Pen, George. (iii. 1349.)
Pennie, or Penny, John. (iii. 1364.)
Pensieu Man's Practice. H. Single-
  ton. 1585. 4to. IV. 294.
Pepwell, Henry. III. 15. (i. 310.)
Perce-forest, ancient French editions
  of this Romance. I. 233.

Perceval, ancient French editions of this Romance. I. 234.

Peregrinatio Humani Generis. Rd. Pynson. 1508. 4to. II. 430.

Perin, or Perrin, John. (iii. 1342.)

Perkins, of the Lawes of England. Rd. Tottel. 1567. 8vo. IV. 437n.

Perotti Grammatica. W. de Worde. 1512. 4to. II. 168.

Pervula. W. de Worde. n.d. 4to. II. 150.

Pervula, Longe. W. de Worde. 1509. 4to. *Ib.*

Peryn's three Sermons. Nichs. Hyll. 1546. 8vo. IV. 231.

Pestilence, Boke of. (Wm. Machlinia.) n.d. 4to. II. 19.

Pestylence, Tretyse agenst. R. Bankes. n.d. 4to. III. 261.

Petit, Thomas. III. 506. (i. 553.)

Petite Pallace. Regd. Wolfe. n.d. 4to. IV. 35.

Petronilla, Life of. Rd. Pynson. n.d. 4to. II. 538.

Phaer's Regiment of Lyfe. Abm. Veale. n.d. 8vo. IV. 368.

Phaer's Virgill. Rowld. Hall. 1562. 4to. IV. 417.

Phillipeis (by H. Junius). T. Berthelet. 1554. 4to. III. 340.

Philosopher's Game. Rowld. Hall. 1563. 8vo. IV. 419.

Philpot's Examination. Hy. Sutton. 1559. 4to. IV. 487.

Phisick, Principal parts of. Edwd. Whitchurch. 1547. 8vo. III. 490.

Phisike, Introduction into. Edw. Whitchurch. n.d. 8vo. III. 501.

Phisiognomie, Art of. John Wayland. n.d. 12mo. III. 532.

Physicke of the Soule. Wm. Hill. 1549. 8vo. IV. 323.

Pierce the Ploughman's Crede. Regd. Wolfe. 1553. 4to. IV. 21.

Pilgrimage of Perfection. Rd. Pynson. 1526. 4to. II. 513.

Pilgrimage of Perfection. W. de Worde. 1531. 4to. II. 288.

Pilgrimage of the Soul. Wm. Caxton. I. 152.

Pilgrimage of the Soul, curious extracts from do. I. 153–158.

Pilgrimage of the Soul, French editions of. I. 159.

Pistels and Gospels. N. Bourman. n.d. 12mo. III. 589.

Pistels and Gospels. J. Herforde. n.d. 4to. III. 559.

Pistels and Gospels. Abm. Veale. n.d. 4to. IV. 369.

Piteous Lamentation. Wm. Powell. 1566. 8vo. IV. 286.

Plage of the Pestilence. J. Gowghe. 1537. 16mo. III. 406.

Plage of the Pestilence, Flying of. Jas. Nicholson. 1537. 16mo. III. 53.

Plague of the Pestilence. L. Askell. n.d. 8vo. III. 587.

Plaie of the Cheastes.. Thos. Marshe. 1569. 8vo. IV. 511.

Plaine Subuersion. H. Singleton. n.d. 32mo. IV. 300.

Plaister for Galled Horse. Thos. Raynald. 1548. 4to. III. 567.

Platforme, perfite, of a Hoppe-garden. Thos. Marshe. 1578. 4to. IV. 526.

Play called the four P. John Allde. 1569. 8vo. IV. 573.

Play of Loue, &c. Wm. Rastell. 1533. fol. III. 376.

Potacion for Lent. J. Gowghe.
1542. 12mo. III. 410n.
1543. 8vo. III. 412.
Powell, Humphrey. IV. 310. (ii. 749.)
Powell, or Powel, Thomas. IV. 543. (ii. 874.)
Powell, William. IV. 281. (ii. 735.)
Power of God's Worde. Thos. Raynald. 1548. 16mo. III. 568.
Praat, William, a Friend of Caxton. I. 265.
Practise of a Papist with a young Maid. Rt. Walley. 1582. 4to. IV. 278.
Prayer, Book of Common. Rd. Grafton. 1549. fol. III. 463.
    1550. 4to. III. 469.
    1552. fol. III. 475.
    1559. fol. III. 482n.
Prayer, Booke of Common. Edw. Whitchurch.
1552. 8vo. III. 498n.
n.d. 4to. III. 499.
Prayer, Fourme of, &c., at Geneva. 1550. 8vo. III. 497.
Prayer, Forme of. Rd. Jugge.
1563. 4to. IV. 254.
1572. 4to. IV. 258.
n.d. 8vo. IV. 262.
Prayer for Queen Mary. John Cawood.
1554. IV. 392.
n.d. broadside. IV. 403n.
Prayer, Godlie and Zealous. H. Singleton. n.d. broadside. IV. 300.
Prayer, or Supplycacion, by Pyttes. Wm. Herforde. 1559. single sheet. III. 562.
Prayer sayd by the Lorde Sturton. Thos. Marshe. 1557. IV. 497n.

Prayers, Booke of Common. Edw. Whitchurch. 1549. fol. III. 493.
Prayers, Manual of. John Wayland.
1539. 4to. III. 518.
1539. 8vo. III. 519.
Prayers of Holy Fathers. Rt. Redman. n.d. 12mo. III. 244n.
Prayers or Meditations. John Wayland. 1545. 16mo. III. 520.
Prayers or Medytacyons. T. Berthelet. 1545. 8vo. III. 329.
    1545. 8vo. III. 330.
Prayse and Commendations. Ay. Scoloker. n.d. 16mo. IV. 307.
Prayse of Women. John Kynge. n.d. 4to. IV. 340n.
Preacher, The. Thos. Marshe. 1574. 8vo. IV. 518.
Preceptes, &c., Transl. by Paynell. T. Berthelet. n.d. 12mo. III. 347n.
Precepts of Cato. John Tysdall. 1560. 16mo. IV. 346.
Preces Privatæ. Wm. Seres.
1568. 12mo. IV. 214.
1573. 12mo. IV. 218.
Preparation to Deathe. T. Berthelet. 1543. 8vo. III. 320.
Preparation to Death. (Erasmus.) T. Berthelet. 1549. 12mo. III. 336n.
Preparation to the Crosse. Thos. Petit. n.d. 16mo. III. 515.
Preseruative agaynst Disperacion. Wm. Copland. 1551. 12mo. III. 132.
Preservative against Poison of Pelagius. Andw. Hester. 1551. 8vo. III. 536.
Presidents, Booke of. Rd. Grafton.
[1546.] 16mo. III. 452.
1550. 8vo. III. 473.

Proclamation against Clipped Money. W. Faques. [1504.] broadside. III. 7.

Proclamation concerning eating Flesh. Rd. Jugge. 1559. 4to. IV. 248.

Proclamation of Jesus Christ, &c. John Allde. 1577. 8vo. IV. 576n.

Proclamation on the Decease of Q. Mary. Rd. Jugge. 1558. IV. 247.

Proclamation. T. Berthelet. 1541, &c. single sheets. III. 316, 319, 324, 331, 346. 1530. single sheet. III. 274. 1536. single sheet. III. 292. 1538. single sheet. III. 302.

Proclamation. John Cawood. 1553-4. broadside. IV. 390n. 1556. broadside. IV. 397n. 1558-60. broadside. IV. 399n. 1562. 4to. IV. 401.

Proclamation. Rd. Grafton. 1541. III. 444. 1548. III. 463n. 1550, &c. III. 473. See also pages 457n, 467n, 475.

Proclamation. Edw. Whitchurch. III. 485n.

Proclamation of Lady Jane Grey. Rd. Grafton. 1553. fol. III. 481.

Proclamation of Queen Mary. 1553. fol. III. 481.

Profit of Enmyes. T. Berthelet. n.d. 8vo. III. 347.

Profitable Book for Man's Soul. W. de Worde. n.d. fol. II. 298.

Prognosticacyon of Thybault. John Rastell. 1533. III. 98.

Prognostication for 1550. Thos. Raynald. [1549.] 8vo. III. 570n.

Prognostication of Erra Pater. Rt. Wyer. n.d. 12mo. III. 196.

Prognostication, &c., of Two Shepherdes. n.d. 12mo. III. 197.

Prognostication from Ypocras, &c. n.d. 12mo. III. 197.

Prognostications for M.D.XLVI. Rd. Grafton. 1546. 12mo. III. 452n.

Promptorium Parvulorum. J. Notary. n.d. 4to. II. 585.

Promptorius Puerorum. Rd. Pynson. 1499. fol. II. 416.

Promptuarium Parvulorum. W. de Worde. 1510. 4to. II. 155.

Properties of Medicine. W. de Worde. n.d. 4to. II. 305.

Propositions of Articles. Rd. Jugge. 1568. 8vo. IV. 256.

Propugnaculum Sacerdot. Evangel. Rd. Pynson. 1523 or 4. 4to. II. 51.

Protestation, &c. T. Berthelet. 1537. 4to. III. 298.

Protestation of French Ambassador. Rd. Jugge. 1560. 4to. IV. 251.

Protestation, Responce à la. Rd. Jugge. 1560. 4to. III. 251.

Proude Wyues Pater Noster. John Kynge. 1560. 4to. IV. 338.

Prymer, first edition of. I. 58.*

Prymer, Engl. and Lat. Rt. Redman. 1537. 8vo. III. 231.

Prymer in Englysshe. J. Byddel. [1534]. 8vo. III. 388. 1535. 8vo. III. 389.

Prymer of Salisbery Use. J. Gowghe. 1536. 8vo. III. 403.

Prymer of Salisbury Use. Rt. Toy. 1541. 8vo. III. 574.

Pryncyples of Astronomye. Rt. Copland. n.d. 4to. III. 125.

Pynson, Richard. II. i. 401. (i. 238.)

Pynson, Richard, his typographical taste. I. x. cxxvi.

Pype, or Toune, of Life of Perfection. Rt. Redman. 1532. 4to. III. 224.

Pyramus and Thisbe. Thos. Hacket. n.d. 4to. IV. 588n.

Pysteles and Gospeles. Wm. Hill. n.d. 4to. IV. 323.

Quatuor Sermones. Wm. Caxton. I. 161, 170.

Quatuor Sermones, copious extracts from do. I. 172, &c.

Quatuor Sermones. J. Notary. [1499.] fol. II. 576.

Quatuor Sermones. W. de Worde. 1493. 4to. II. 33, &c.

Questionary of Cyrurgyens. Rt. Wyer. 1541. 4to. III. 180.

Quintus Curtius. Rd. Tottel. 1553. 4to. IV. 424n. 1561. 4to. IV. 432.

Ramsay's Comfortable Communication, &c. Rd. Day. 1585. 8vo. IV. 182.

Ramsay's Communications, &c. John Day. n.d. 8vo. IV. 173.

Raoul Le Fevre, his Recueil des Histoires de Troye. I. lxxxv. 2.

Raoul Le Fevre, Caxton's translation of ditto. I. lxxxv. 16.

Raoul Le Fevre, ancient French editions of. I. 11.

Rastell, John. III. 81. (i. 326.)

Rastell, William. III. 370. (i. 473.)

Rastell; Collection of Statutes. Rd. Tottel. 1557. 4to. IV. 430. 1574. 4to. IV. 444.

Ratdolt, the foreign printer, mention of. I. vi, xl.

Rates of Customs, &c. Rd. Kele. 1545. IV. 302.

Rates of Watermen, &c. John Cawood. n.d. IV. 404, 403n.

Raynald, Thomas. III. 363. (i. 581.)

Raynalde's Birth of Mankind, facsimile of a print. I. xxv.

Raynalde's Birth of . Mankynde. Wm. Seres. n.d. 4to. IV. 222.

Raynarde the Foxe. Thos. Gualtier. 1550. 8vo. IV. 342.

Reconyng, Famouse kepyng of. J. Gowghe. 1543. 4to. III. 415.

Redborne, Robert IV. 196. (ii. 686.)

Redman, Elizabeth. III. 248.

Redman, John. III. 59. (iii. 1451.)

Redman, Robert. III. 213. (i. 385.)

Reformatio Legum Eccles. John Day. 1571. 4to. IV. 122.

Regal and Ecclesiastical Power. Wm. Copland. 1548. 12mo. III. 130. n.d. 12mo. III. 152.

Regimen Principum. W. de Worde. n.d. 4to. II. 344.

Regimen Sanitatis Salerni. T. Berthelet. 1535. 4to. III. 292.

Regimen Sanitatis Salerni. Abm. Veale. 1557. 16mo. and 8vo. IV. 360n. 1558. 8vo. and 4to. IV. 360n. 1575. 8vo. IV. 363.

Regiment for the Sea. Thos. Hacket. n.d. 4to. IV. 588.

Regiment for the Sea. John Wight. 1584. 4to. IV. 375. n.d. 4to. IV. 379.

Sepulveda de Ritu Nuptiarum, &c.
John Cawood. 1553. 4to. IV.
390.
Seraphicall Dirge. J. Byddel. n.d.
8vo. III. 399n.
Seres, William. IV. 193. (ii. 686.)
Sergier, or Sergyr, Richard.
(iii. 1336.)
Serll, or Scerlle, Richard. (ii. 964.)
Sermo Alcock. W. de Worde. n.d.
8vo. II. 343.
Sermo Fratris Hieronymi. Rd.
Pynson. 1509. 4to. II. 438.
Sermo pro Episcopo Puerorum. W.
de Worde. n.d. 4to. II. 379.
Sermon. Wm. Hill. n.d. 8vo. IV.
322n.
Sermon (by Bp. Fisher). T. Berthe-
let. n.d. 4to. III. 343.
Sermon by Colet. n.d. 8vo. III.
344.
Sermon, made in 1388. John Kynge.
n.d. IV. 339.
Sermon, Notable. G. Lynne. 1550.
8vo. IV. 317.
Sermon of Vrbane Regius. John
Day. 1578. 4to. IV. 148.
Sermon preached at St. Paul's
Cross. Rd. Pynson. n.d. 4to.
II. 545.
Sermones Barones. W. de Worde.
n.d. 4to. II. 343.
Sermones Discipuli. J. Notary.
1510. 4to. II. 583.
Sermons. John Tysdall. n.d. 8vo.
IV. 352.
Sermons appointed by the Queen.
Rd. Jugge. 1559. 4to. IV. 249.
1563. 4to. IV. 253.
Sermons, Fulke's. John Awdely.
1571. 16mo. IV. 565.
1574. 8vo. IV. 566.

Sermons, Dering's. John Awdely.
1569. 16mo. IV. 565n.
Sermons, Bedal's. John Awdely.
1571. 16mo. IV. 565n.
Sermons found hid in a wall. John
Awdely. 1573. 8vo. IV. 566n.
1575. 8vo. IV. 568.
Sermons, Crowley's. John Awdely.
1575. 8vo. IV. 567.
Sermons, Bradforde's. John Awdely.
1574. IV. 569n.
Sermons, Bush's. John Awdely.
1571. 8vo. IV. 569n.
Sermons, Brokis's. Rt. Caley.
1554-5. 8vo. IV. 458.
Sermons, Fisher's. Rt. Caley. 1554.
8vo. IV. 458.
Sermon, a Fruitful and Godly.
Rt. Caley. 1554. 16mo. IV.
459.
Sermons, Glaziers. Rt. Caley. 1555.
8vo. IV. 461.
Sermons, Fakenham's. Rt. Caley.
1555. 8vo. IV. 461.
Sermons, Harpsfield's. Rt. Caley.
1556. 16mo. IV. 463.
Sermons, Edgeworth's. Rt. Caley.
1557. 4to and 8vo. IV. 463.
Sermons, Godly and Notable. J.
Herforde. n.d. 8vo. III. 559.
Sermons of St. Augustine. John
Cawood. 1555. 8vo. IV. 394.
Sermons upon the Apocalipse. John
Day. 1573. 4to. IV. 131.
Setoni Dialecta. Thos. Marshe.
1572. 8vo. IV. 517.
1577. 8vo. IV. 524.
Seuen Wyse Maysters of Rome. W.
Copland. n.d. 8vo. III. 170.
Seven Sheddings of Christ's Blood.
W. de Worde. 1509. 4to. II.
143.

Smith, Richard, some account of.
I. lxxiv.
Smith, Toby. (ii. 1306.)
Smyth, Answere to Maister. R.
Bankes. n.d. 4to. III. 260.
Smyth, Henry. IV. 227. (ii. 706.)
Smyth, whych forged him a new dame.
Wm. Copland. n.d. 4to. III.
157.
Smythe's Defence of the Masse.
Wm. Middleton. 1547. 8vo. III.
550.
Smythe's Sermon. Rd. Tottel.
1572. IV. 441n.
Smyth's Bukler of Catholyke Fayeth.
Rt. Cayley. 1558. 8vo. IV. 461.
Smythicke, or Smethwicke, John.
(iii. 1384.)
Socrates, his satire against the Fair
Sex incorporated by Caxton in his
Dictes and Sayings. I. 66–69.
Solace of the Soule. Wm. Hill.
1548. 8vo. IV. 322n.
Solmpne, Anthony de. (iii. 1462.)
Solomon, Canticles or Balades of.
T. Berthelet. 1549. 12mo. III.
336n.
Solomon, Sayings and Proverbs of.
Rd. Pynson. n.d. 4to. II. 567.
Sommarie de la Graunde Abridge-
ment. Rd. Tottel. 1565. sm. fol.
IV. 425.
Song of the Chyld Byshop. John
Cawood. 1555. 4to. IV. 394.
Song of the Lorde's Supper. Rt.
Stoughton. IV. 314.
Spare your Good. Anty. Kytson.
n.d. 4to. IV. 542.
Spectacle of Lovers. W. de Worde.
n.d. 4to. II. 337.
Speculum Christiani. Wm. Mach-
linia. n.d. 4to. II. 13.

Speculum Historiale, &c., of Vin-
centius Bellovacensis. I. 257.
Speculum Spiritualium. Hy. Pepwell.
1510. fol. III. 21.
Speculum Vitæ Christi. Wm. Caxton.
I. 320.
Spiritual and precious Pearle. H.
Singleton.
1569. 16mo. IV. 292n.
n.d. 16mo. IV. 297.
Spiritual Parle, &c. John Allde.
n.d. small. IV. 577.
Spiritual Perle. John Cawood. 1550.
IV. 387.
Spiritual Purgation, &c. H. Singleton.
n.d. 8vo. IV. 296.
Spiritualitie and Temporalitie. Rt.
Redman. n.d. 8vo. III. 245.
Spirituall and precious Perle. G.
Lynne. 1550. 16mo. IV. 318.
Spirituall Exercises. John Walley.
1557. 8vo. IV. 272.
Spiritus est Vicarius, &c. John
Kingston. 1571. 4to. IV.
475.
Splinter, Merry Jest of. J. Notary.
n.d. 4to. II. 587.
Squyre of Lowe Degre. Wm. Cop-
land. n.d. 4to. III. 164.
Staffe of Christen Faith. John Day.
1577. 8vo. IV. 143.
Stafford, Simon. (ii. 1299.)
Stanbrigi Vocabula. P. Treveris.
n.d. 4to. III. 46.
Stanbrigi Parvulorum Institutio. P.
Treveris. n.d. 4to. III. 46.
Stanbrigi Accidentia. P. Treveris.
n.d. 4to. III. 47.
Stanbrigi Idem Opus. P. Treveris.
n.d. 4to. III. 47.
Stanbrigiana Accidentia. John
Rastell. n.d. 4to. III. 108.

Stoughton, Robert. IV. 312. (ii. 750.)

Stow's Chronicle abridged. Thos. Marshe. 1565. 8vo. IV. 502.

Stow's Summarie of Chronicles. Rd. Tottel. 1575. 8vo. IV. 445.

Strong Battery, &c. Thos. Hacket. 1562. IV. 582n.

Stultifera Navis. John Cawood. 1570. folio. IV. 401.

Success of Famagosta. John Day. 1572. 4to. IV. 125.

Sulpitii Verulami. Rd. Pynson. 1494. 4to. II. 403.

Sum Es Fui. T. Godfray. n.d. 4to. III. 72.

Summe of Christianitie, by Revell. Rt. Redman. n.d. 8vo. III. 229n.

Summe of Divinitie. John Awdely. 1567. 16mo. IV. 564.

Summe of Holy Signes. Rowld. Hall. 1563. 8vo. IV. 418n.

Summe of the Byble. Rt. Stoughton. n.d. 8vo. IV. 314.

Summe of the Holy Scripture. Wm. Hill. 1548. 8vo. IV. 322.

Summe of the Holy Scripture. John Day. 1547. 8vo. IV. 48.

Supper of the Lorde. Rt. Crowley. n.d. 8vo. IV. 334.

Supplycacyon to Henry viii. J. Byddel. 1534. 4to. III. 387.

Supplycacyon of Soulys. Wm. Rastell. n.d. fol. III. 382.

Supplycation to the Quene's Maiestie. John Cawood. [1555.] 8vo. IV. 396.

Surgeri, the Worke of, by I. of Brunswyk. P. Treveris. 1525. fol. III. 35.

Surrey's Poems. Rd. Tottel. 1557. 4to. IV. 430.

Surueying, Boke of. Wm. Copland. n.d. 8vo. III. 147.

Surveying, Boke of. Wm. Middleton. n.d. 8vo. III. 552.

Surveyinge, Boke of. T. Berthelet. 1539. 8vo. III. 305n.

1545. 8vo. III. 328.

1545. 8vo. III. 332.

n.d. 8vo. III. 348.

Sutton, Edward. (iii. 1309.)

Sutton, Henry. IV. 485. (ii. 843.)

Sweynkeym and Pannartz; their Petition to Pope Paul II. I. 11.

Sycke Man's Salve. John Day. 1561. 8vo. IV. 79.

Symbolœographia. Rd. Tottel. 1590. 4to. IV. 454.

Syr Beuys of Hampton. Wm. Copland. n.d. 4to. III. 165.

Syr Degore. W. Copland. n.d. 4to. III. 164.

Syr Degore. John Kynge. 1560. 4to. IV. 338.

Syr Eglamour of Artoys. W. Copland. n.d. 4to. III. 167.

Syr Isenbras. W. Copland. n.d. 4to. III. 147.

Syr Tryamour. W. Copland. n.d. 4to. III. 164.

Tab, Henry. III. 502. (i. 550.)

Table of Matters in the Bible. Thos. Raynald. n.d. 16mo. III. 568n.

Table of Principal Matters, &c. Wm. Hill. 1548. IV. 322n.

Table of the Statutes. Rd. Tottel. [1570.] fol. IV. 440.

Table of Yeres. John Walley. 1558. 8vo. IV. 273.

Testamentum Novum, Erasmi. Thos. Marshe. 1573. 8vo. IV. 517n.

Testamentum Novum, Lat. John Mayler. 1540. 4to. III. 542.

Testamentum Novum. Thos. Gualtier. 1551. 8vo. IV. 343.

Testimonie of Antiquitie. John Day. 1567. 8vo. IV. 105.

Textus Alexandri. Rd. Pynson. 1505. 4to. II. 426.

Thanksgiving, Form of. Rd. Jugge. 1563. 4to IV. 254.

Theatre, Le. John Day. 1568. 8vo. IV. 107.

Theatrum Mundi. Thos. Hacket. 1574. 16mo. IV. 583.

Theatrum Mundi. John Wight. 1581. 8vo. IV. 374.

Theloall's Digest. Rd. Tottel. 1579. 8vo. IV. 448.

Theodoli Liber. Rd. Pynson. n.d. 4to. II. 537.

Theodoli Liber. W. de Worde. 1515. 4to. II. 208.

Therentii Vulgaria. (Wm. Machlinia.) n.d. 4to. II. 20.

Thersytes, New Enterlude of. John Tysdall. n.d. 4to. IV. 352.

Thomas, St., Life of. Rd. Pynson. n.d. 4to. II. 555.

Thomas's Italian Grammar. Thos. Powell. 1561. 4to. IV 545n.

Thomas's Vanity of the World. T. Berthelet. 1545. 8vo. III. 331.

Thomas's Historie of Italy. T. Berthelet. 1549. 4to. III. 334.

Thomas's Italian Grammar. T. Berthelet. 1550. 4to. III. 336.

Thomasius, or Thomas, Thomas. (iii. 1414.)

Three Godly Sermons, &c. Rt. Toy. 1546. 8vo. III. 574.

Thucydides, by Nicolls. John Wayland. 1550. fol. III. 520.

Thyestes, by Jasper Heywood. T. Berthelet. 1560. 12mo. III. 352.

Tilly, William. IV. 341. (ii. 764.)

Tiptoft, Earl of Worcester, some account of. I. 127.

Tiptoft, Earl of Worcester, Caxton's character of. I. cxvii. 127.

Tirannie of the Papistes. Wm. Seres. 1562. 8vo. IV. 207.

Titus and Gisippus. Thos. Hacket. 1562. 4to. IV. 581.

Titus and Gesyppus. W. de Worde. n.d. 4to. II. 338.

Touney's Rules of Grammar. Rd. Pynson. n.d. 8vo. II. 539.

Tonstallus, in Laud Matrimonii. Rd. Pynson. 1518. 4to. II. 478, &c.

Tonstallus de Arte Supputandi. Rd. Pynson. 1522. 4to. *Ib.*

Too late married. W. de Worde. n.d. 4to. II. 386.

Too soon married. W. de Worde. n.d. 4to. II. 384.

Tor; one of the Knights of the Round Table. 1. 250.

Tottel, Richard. IV. 422. (ii. 806.)

Touchstone for the Time. Thos. Hacket. 1574. 8vo. IV. 584.

Touchstone of Complexions. Thos. Marshe. 1576. 8vo. IV. 522.

Toxaris of Lucian. Hy. Sutton. 1565. 8vo. IV. 489.

Toxophilus. Edw. Whitchurch. 1545. 4to. III. 486.

Toy, Humphrey. (ii. 933.)

Toy, Robert. III. 573. (i. 585.)

Toy, Widow of. III. 577. (i. 588.)

Treatise on the Church. John
Cawood. 1556. 8vo. IV. 398n.

Treatise on the Pope's Supremacie.
Hy. Sutton. 1560. 8vo. IV. 485.

Treatise or Sermon. G. Lynne.
1550. 8vo. IV. 317.

Treatyse of Thassocation. Rowld.
Hall. 1562. 8vo. IV. 413.

Tretise, Behouefull. T. Gibson.
1536. 4to. III. 401.

Treveris, Peter. III. 31. (iii.
1441.)

Treveris, Peter, his typographical
skill. I. xii.

Treveris, Peter, engraved fac-similes
from his edition of the Poly-
chronicon. I. xiii., xv.

Trevisa, John De, some account of.
I. 140, 141.

Treviso, John De, whether he translated the Bible. I. 142.

Trew Judgement of a Faithful
Chrystyan. Rt. Stoughton. n.d.
16mo. IV. 313.

Triades, or Trinities of Rome. T.
Godfray. n.d. 8vo. III. 69.

Triall of the Supremacy. Thos.
Marshe. 1556. 8vo. IV. 496.

Tristan or Tristrem, ancient French
editions of this Romance. I. 233.

Tritameron of Love. John Kingston.
1584. 4to. IV. 483.

Troas, a Tragedy. Rd. Tottel. 1560.
16mo. IV. 432n.

Troilus and Cresside. Wm. Caxton.
I. 313.

Troilus and Cresseide. W. de Worde.
1517. 4to. II. 212.

Troubled Man's Medicine. John
Allde. 1567. 8vo. IV. 572.

Troubled Man's Medicine. J. Herforde. 1546. 8vo. III. 558.

Troubled Man's Medicine. Owen
Rogers. n.d. small. IV. 547.

Troy, History of the Siege of. Rd.
Pynson. 1513. fol. II. 447.

Troy, Receuylle of the Histories
of. W. Copland. 1553. fol. III.
133.

Troy, Recueil des Histoires de.
Caxton's French edition. I. 2.

Troy, Recueil des Histoires de, description of an ancient MS. of.
I. 5.

Troy, Recueil des Histoires de, ditto,
English edition. I. 16.

Troy, Recueil des Histoires de.
Specimen of ditto. I. 24.

Troy, Recueil of the Siege of. W. de
Worde. 1503. fol. II. 115.

True Copies of Letters. John Day.
1560. 8vo. IV. 77.

Truthall, Christopher. III. 60. (iii.
1451.)

Tryumphs of Petrarcke. John
Cawood. n.d. IV. 404.

Tullius Offices. J. Byddel. 1540.
12mo. III. 396.

Tullius De Senectute. J. Byddel.
1540. 12mo. III. 396.
n.d. 8vo. III. 397.

Tully's Offices. W. de Worde.
1534. 8vo. II. 293.

Tully, of Old Age and Friendship.
Wm. Caxton. I. 119.

Tunstall, Letter by, to Cardinal Pole.
Regd. Wolfe. 1560. 8vo. IV. 25.

Tunstall's Prayers. John Cawood.
1555. 16mo. IV. 399.

Turk, John. IV. 357. (ii. 771.)

Turke's Chronicle. Edw. Whitchurch. 1546. 8vo. III. 488.

Turler's Traveiler. Abm. Veale.
1575. 16mo. IV. 362.

Vocacyon of Johän Bale. H. Single-
ton. 1553. 8vo. IV. 290.
Voigt, Mr. John. I. 66.*
Voraigne, Jacobus De. I. 190.
Voyce of the last Trumpet. Rt.
Crowley. 1549. 8vo. IV. 327.
Vpcheringe of the Messe. John Day.
n.d. 12mo. IV. 171.
Upton, Nicholas, de re Militari. W.
de Worde. 1496. fol. II. 69.
Vrinal of Physick. Regd. Wolfe.
1548. 8vo. IV. 10.
1567. 8vo. IV. 31.
Vrynes, Seinge of. Wm. Middleton.
1544. 16mo. III. 548.
Vrynes, Seynge of. R. Bankes.
1525. 4to. III. 251.
Vrynes, Seynge of. Eliz. Redman.
n.d. 8vo. III. 249.
Vrynes, The Seinge of. W. Copland.
1552. 12mo. III. 133.
Vrynes, The Seynge of. Rt. Redman.
n.d. 8vo. III. 241.
n.d. 8vo. III. 249.
Vulgarii Hormanni. W. de Worde.
1530. 4to. II. 286.

Wakefield, Roberti, de laud. Linguar.
W. de Worde. 1524. 4to. II. 254.
Waldegrave or Walgrave, Robert.
(ii. 1139.)
Walley, John. IV. 269. (ii. 729.)
Walley, Robert. IV. 278. (ii. 734.)
Walsh, John, his Examination. John
Awdely. 1566 8vo. IV. 531.
Ward, Roger. (ii. 1189.)
Warning against Papistes. John Day.
n.d. 8vo. IV. 165.
Warning to the Wise. John Allde.
1580. 8vo. IV. 576.
Watchword for Wilful Women. Thos.
Marshe. 1581. 8vo. IV. 531.

Watchworde to Englande. Thos.
Hacket. 1584. 4to. IV. 584.
Water Marks. I. cxxv., with plates.
Waterson, Simon. (ii. 1222.)
Watkins, Richard. (ii. 1023.)
Watson's Sermons. John Cawood.
1554. 4to. IV. 393n.
Way to Wealth. Rt. Crowley. 1550.
8vo. IV. 330.
Wayland, John. III. 516. (i. 558.)
Webster or Webber, Richard. (ii.
1138.)
Welchmen, of their ancient Manners
and Rites. I. 146.
Well Sprynge of Sciences. Rowld.
Hall. 1562. 16mo. IV. 416.
Wenefrid, Life of St. Wm. Caxton.
I. 341.
Werke for Housholders. Rt. Redman.
1531. 12mo. III. 220.
1537. 8vo. III. 231–244.
Werk of Preparation. Rt. Redman.
n.d. 8vo. III. 240.
Werburg, St., Life of. Rd. Pynson.
1521. 4to. II. 491.
Werner, Rolewinck de Laer. I. 149.
Weston, Hugonis, Oratio. Rt. Caley.
1553. 8vo. IV. 457n.
Whetstone of Witte. John Kingston.
1557. 4to. IV. 467.
Whital's Short Dictionary. W. de
Worde. n.d. 4to. II. 323.
Whitchurch, Edward. III. 483. (i.
539.)
White or Whyte, Edward. (ii.
1197.)
White, William, and Gabriel Simson.
(ii. 1263.)
White, William. (ii. 1266.)
Whitintoni Opuscula Grammatica.
Rd. Pynson. [1515.] 4to. II.
449–454.

Wykes, or Wekes, Henry. (ii. 937.)
Wyl Buck's Testament. W. Copland.
n.d. 4to. III. 156.
Wynkyn de Worde : his typographical
skill. viii. cxxvi.
Wysdome, Boke of. Rt. Wyer. 1532.
12mo. III. 175.
Wyse, or Wise, Andrew. (iii. 1372.)

Xenophon, VIII. Bookes of. Regd.
Wolfe. 1567. 8vo. IV. 31.
n.d. 8vo. IV. 35.
Xenophon, Treatise of Householde.
John Allde. 1573. 8vo. IV. 574n.
Xenophon, Treatise of Householde.
T. Berthelet. [1534.] 8vo. III.
288.
Xenophon, Treatise of Householde.
Abm. Veale. 1557. IV. 360n.

Yarath, James. (iii. 1351.)
Yardley, Richard. (ii. 1205.)
Year Books. T. Berthelet. 1532.
fol. III. 279.
Year Books. Wm. Middleton. n.d.
fol. III. 553n.
Year Books. John Rastell. n.d. fol.
III. 110.
Year Books. Rd. Pynson. 1517 to
1520. fol. II. 473.
Year Books. I. to VIII. Hen. VII.
Rt. Redman.
1525. fol. III. 218n.
n.d. fol. III. 229n.
Year Books. XIX. Edw. IV. Rt.
Redman. 1527. fol. III. 219n.
Year Books. Temp. Edw. III. Rt.
Redman. n.d. fol. III. 240n.

Year Books for 9 Hen. IV. Rt.
Wyer. n.d. fol. III. 188.
Year Books. Hen. VI. Wm.
Machlinia. n.d. fol. II. 9, 10.
Year Books. Hen. VII. Rd. Tottel.
1555. 8vo. IV. 426.
Year Books. Edw. V. and Hen. VII.
Rd. Tottel. 1555. fol. IV. 428.
Year Books. Hen. VI. and Edw. III.
Rd. Tottel. 1556. fol. IV. 430.
Year Books. Edw. III. Rd. Tottel.
1561. fol. IV. 432n.
Year Books. Edw. III. Rd. Tottel.
1576. fol. IV. 446.
Year Books. Hen. VII. and Edw. III.
Rd. Tottel. 1583-5. fol. IV. 451.
Year Books. Richard III. Rd.
Tottel. 1587. fol. IV. 453n.
Year Books. Hen. VIII. Rd. Tottel.
1591. fol. IV. 454n.
Yetsweirt, Charles. (ii. 1130.)
Ymage of Both Churches. John
Wyer. 1550. 4to. IV. 240.
Ymage of Both Churches. Rd. Wyer.
1550. 12mo. IV. 239.
Ymage of bothe Pastoures. Rd. Kele.
1550. IV. 303n.
Yny Ihyvyr. Edw. Whitchurch.
1546. 8vo. III. 488.
Young, William. (iii. 1357.)
Ypodigma Neustriæ. John Day.
1574. fol. IV. 136.

Zel Ulric, short account of his early
printing. I. xc.
Zodyake of Lyfe. John Tysdall.
1560. 8vo. IV. 346.
1561. 16mo. IV. 347.

www.ingramcontent.com/pod-product-compliance
Lightning Source LLC
Chambersburg PA
CBHW020313090426
42735CB00009B/1326